RURAL RITES

Hunting and the Politics of Prejudice

Charlie Pye-Smith

**ALL PARTY PARLIAMENTARY
MIDDLE WAY GROUP**

2006

First published
in Great Britain in 2006 by the
All Party Parliamentary Middle Way Group
House of Commons, London SW1A 0AA

Copyright © Charlie Pye-Smith

Charlie Pye-Smith has asserted his right
to be identified as the author of this work

ISBN 0 9552384 0 4
ISBN 978 0 9552384 0 6

Design and typesetting by *designsection*
(part of Butler and Tanner Ltd)
Printing and binding by Butler and Tanner Ltd,
Frome and London

Set in Monotype Perpetua

FSC

Mixed Sources
Product group from well-managed
forests and other controlled sources

Cert no. SGS-COC-1722
www.fsc.org
© 1996 Forest Stewardship Council

*The pages in this book have been
printed on paper certified in accordance
with the rules of the
Forest Stewardship Council*

'Bad laws are the worst sort of tyranny.'

Edmund Burke

★

'It requires very little knowledge to care
passionately about animals. It requires
a great deal of understanding to care
properly for them.'

John Webster
Animal Welfare – Limping Towards Eden

CONTENTS

ACKNOWLEDGEMENTS

Many people have provided me with help and information during the research and writing of *Rural Rites*. It seems invidious to mention so few among so many, but I would particularly like to thank Peter Oborne for writing the foreword, Alexander Ashworth for helping with the book design and printing, Carrie May for designing the cover illustration and Harry Boggis-Rolfe for his legal advice. Very special thanks must go to Richard Schuster and the individuals whose generosity made all this possible. The All Party Parliamentary Middle Way Group, which commissioned this study, is greatly indebted to Richard Schuster.

by *Peter Oborne* Political Editor of *The Spectator*

On February 18th 2005 it suddenly became much more dangerous to be a fox, a hare or a deer, the three species most affected by the ban on hunting with dogs. Their chances of living a long, comfortable life were sharply reduced. Their prospects of suffering a long, lingering death through snaring, poisoning or wounding were very much increased. Thousands of hares, for example, were shot by farmers during the months immediately after the Hunting Act became law. They had been tolerated as a pest on account of coursing, but there is now no incentive for hard-pressed farmers to keep a healthy hare population alive in their fields. Some farmers would hold back from using pesticides in order to sustain their hare population, and have now taken up the practice once again.

No huntsman, no matter how relentless or bloodthirsty, has ever done a fraction as much damage to the cause of small, furry mammals as the Labour MPs Gerald Kaufman and his friend the late Tony Banks, who memorably ended his days as Lord Stratford. The paradox is that Kaufman, Banks and their anti-hunting allies claimed to be concerned about animal welfare. Their Hunting Act is a dramatic example of the law of unintended consequences. Rather as George Bush's 'war on terror' has provided a marvellous boost for Al Q'aeda, enabling it to flourish and gain converts in places where previously it did not even exist, so the Hunting Act has proved catastrophic for the interests of the very creatures it was designed to protect.

This book is the first serious attempt to provide a measured account of the wretched events leading up to the Hunting Act. It is fair minded, and at times more critical than many would appreciate of the Countryside Alliance and others in the hunting world. The author Charlie Pye-Smith is scrupulous, measured in his judgment, and exceptionally well informed. He writes in a clear and easy style. His book is not simply about hunting by any means: it has a much broader application than that. Pye-Smith is an essential read for anyone who wishes to understand how Britain is governed at the start of the 21st century.

Viewed from this perspective Pye-Smith's book is terrifying. It demonstrates that we are ruled by emotion rather than logic, by ignorance rather than knowledge, by bigotry rather than under-standing. He shows that we now live in something approaching a totalitarian state, where the reasoned arguments of a minority are powerless against the prejudice of the majority.

Pye-Smith's over-riding explanation for the calamity of the Hunt-ing Act is very important. The MPs who sponsored the legislation were fundamentally uninterested in animal welfare. Their prime objective was something else. As Llin Golding, a pro-hunting Labour peer, noted: 'it was all about pay-back time for the miners.'

This largely hidden objective explains many things that are other-wise mysterious. It accounts for the lack of real concern for animal welfare behind the Hunting Act. It accounts for the fact that the antis are apparently undisturbed by fishing, which has no wider purpose beyond human pleasure, but viciously opposed to hunting, which is often justified by the need for pest control in rural areas.

Above all it explains why the anti-hunters were almost incapable of being moved by argument. A very few MPs, to their credit, did pay attention to the 700 hours of debate which took place in Parliament. Labour's Barry Sheerman, for example, listened to the facts, changed his mind, and made a speech suggesting to colleagues they should climb out of the 'trenches of prejudice'. But for the large part the facts had nothing to do with the arguments. Indeed the antis were almost wholly disreputable in the way they made their case.

That was only to be expected. Pye-Smith shows, unfortunately, that government ministers were also unscrupulous. One of the most powerful sections of the book lays bare Rural Affairs Minister Alun Michael's collaboration with the pro-ban lobby during the Portcullis House hearings. Many of us had been prepared to accept that Alun Michael, though an ineffective minister, had at least been fair in his handling of the Bill. Pye-Smith produces compelling evidence to show that Michael succumbed to pressure from the antis.

The most important part of the book deals with the habitual misuse of evidence by anti-hunting bodies. The experience of the Nazis in the 1930s and Stalinism in the 1940s has shown how science can be abused for political purposes. The debate over hunting shows that the lesson has still not been learnt. In Chapter Two, Pye-Smith exposes the tricks, fabrication and deceit used by the massively well funded animal welfare lobby to win their arguments. He shows how even apparently reputable bodies like the National Trust, and incorruptible figures like high court judges, can be convinced by biased or partial material. The evidence he produces fully supports his conclusion that the animal rights movement 'launched their tendentious findings at a party political conference; they used them in public forums; they undoubtedly influenced the political process. This is a clear example of the corruption of science for political purposes'.

This book has an application that goes so much further than hunting and animal welfare. It shows us the ease with which bad law can be made, how simple it is to spin the facts, and how readily the rights of minorities can be obliterated. Our little local difficulty over hunting encapsulates many of the great political problems of our time. Charlie Pye-Smith's book deserves a very wide readership indeed.

Rural Rites Wronged

Since 1997, when the Labour government was returned to power with a huge majority, Parliament has spent 700 hours, equivalent to over seventeen 40-hour weeks, debating and taking evidence on whether or not hunting with dogs should be banned. This monumental effort culminated in November 2004 with the passage of the Hunting Act. It is a remarkable piece of legislation. Instead of improving animal welfare – its ostensible aim – it is almost certainly doing the opposite. Furthermore, the Act has alienated a significant chunk of society by proscribing, or attempting to proscribe, an activity enjoyed by tens of thousands of law-abiding citizens.

The Members of Parliament who were primarily responsible for getting the Act on to the statute books have made much of their achievement. For example, Sir Gerald Kaufman, Labour MP for Manchester Gorton, proudly informed his constituents in a newsletter: 'I promised you that I would work for this … Foxes, hare and deer will no longer legally be the prey of the tally-ho mob.' But Kaufman is fooling himself and his constituents: the Act does not ban hunting; it bans certain types of hunting.

You can still hunt rats and rabbits with as many dogs as you wish, and even do so dressed in a red coat and on horseback, but it is illegal to hunt mice and it is illegal to hunt hares – unless, that is, you are in pursuit of a hare which has been shot. You can use terriers to flush a fox from below ground prior to shooting it, providing you are doing so to protect game birds (which will later be shot). But you cannot use terriers to flush out foxes to protect livestock or ground-nesting birds such as golden plover or curlew. Nor can you use terriers below ground to help dispatch an injured or diseased fox, or rescue orphaned cubs. If you deliberately chase a fox above ground with a pack of hounds, you will be breaking the law. But you can flush a fox out of a wood or hedgerow or wherever it takes refuge with one or two dogs, providing you shoot it. Or try to shoot it.

The Act is not about reducing the number of foxes, deer, hare or mink – the principal species hunted with dogs – which are killed each year. Rather, it favours more shooting and less biting; humans, not dogs, are expected to deliver the coup de grace. Those who favoured a ban consistently argued, both inside and outside Parliament, that shooting is a more humane way of killing foxes than hunting. Yet the evidence, ignored by most MPs, suggests the opposite is often true, and there is every reason to believe that the sum total of animal suffering will now increase as result of the Hunting Act.

Seldom can a piece of legislation have been held up to such overt ridicule by those whose activities it is supposed to curtail. There is nothing to stop a huntsman from laying an artificial trail for a pack of hounds – in fact, the pro-banners have long argued that drag hunting provides a good recreational alternative to the hunting of live quarry – and there is nothing to stop these same hounds from independently deciding to pursue, should they came across one, a real fox and do what they have been trained to do: kill it. The huntsman, if questioned by the police, simply has to say something along the lines of: 'It was nothing to do with me, Officer!' In other words, he can claim that it was not his intent that the hounds should divert from an artificial scent to that of a live fox. And who is to say he isn't telling the truth? In reality, it may be very difficult for even a huntsman to know when the hounds have changed from hunting an artificial scent to hunting a live-quarry scent.

Those who campaigned for a ban on hunting, and those who

voted for it, were under the impression that once the Hunting Act
came into force that would be the end of the matter. John Bryant,
a long-serving press and publicity officer of the League Against
Cruel Sports, once predicted that within a couple of months of a
ban everyone would have forgotten what all the fuss was about.[1]
Many of the MPs who voted for a ban thought the same, and they
made no bones about how relieved they were to see the back of a
troublesome and time-consuming issue. The pro-hunting peer
Lord Mancroft recalls meeting a recently ennobled Labour MP
who told him: 'Thank God I'll never have to vote on a hunting bill
again!'. As far as he and many others were concerned, the hunting
issue had been resolved. It was now history.

How wrong they were. Some 300 organised packs of hounds
remain in business and continue to pursue wild animals, many doing
so two or more times a week. To stay on the right side of the law
they have been obliged to change the way they do things, introduce
new practices and demonstrate that it was not their intention to
catch foxes with hounds when they inadvertently do. But they
have made a point, which is that the Hunting Act does not work.
The raucous claims of victory from MPs who voted for the ban,
and the approbation they received from organisations such as the
League Against Cruel Sports, the International Fund for Animal
Welfare (IFAW) and the Royal Society for the Prevention of Cruelty
to Animals (RSPCA), now seem premature and hubristic[2].

The aim of this essay is twofold: first, to analyse how we have
ended up with such an inept and illiberal piece of legislation; and
second, to suggest ways in which we could improve the welfare of
wild animals without sacrificing our civil liberties.

The analysis is divided into three chapters. The first chapter –
'Outlawing Your Enemies' – looks at the political background to
the hunting debate. It argues that a significant number of pro-ban
MPs were motivated by a deep-seated hatred of the sort of people
who hunt, rather than by any great concern for animal welfare.

'For most of the MPs who voted for a ban, it was all about pay-back time for the miners,' says Llin (now Baroness) Golding, one of the small number of Labour MPs to vote consistently against a ban. 'Hunting was portrayed as people in red coats – toffs, mainly – tearing animals apart for sport. That's what got most MPs committed to a ban in the first place.' Some MPs openly admitted that class warfare was their main incentive for introducing a hunting ban.

This is not to suggest that there were no serious debates on the core issues of whether hunting is cruel and whether it is necessary. Two government-initiated processes – an inquiry chaired by Lord Burns and a three-day hearing at Portcullis House organised by Alun Michael, the Minister for Rural Affairs – yielded an enormous wealth of material. This meant that MPs had at their disposal a treasure trove of insights into the arguments for and against hunting. They also had Lord Burns' carefully weighed analysis. Some MPs did their best to consider the evidence as fairly as they could. A few MPs who were previously opposed to hunting even changed their minds. In a rousing speech, Barry Sheerman, Labour MP for Huddersfield, told his colleagues why he no longer believed in a ban and invited them to climb out of the 'trenches of prejudice'. Few took up the offer.

Kate Hoey, Labour MP for Vauxhall and an articulate champion of licensed hunting – she was appointed chair of the Countryside Alliance while I was writing this essay – describes the third reading of the Hunting Act as the most depressing event in her long political career. That day the virtues which have helped to define our democracy – a respect for the beliefs of others, a refusal to countenance obfuscation and lies, the courage to grapple with difficult issues – were swept away by a tide of ignorance and bigotry. A relatively small number of committed anti-hunting MPs, marshalled by Tony Banks (then Labour MP for West Ham), were followed into the 'aye' lobby by a great army of MPs who had seldom or never listened to the debates (there were occasions when as few as 25 remained in the chamber), never reflected on other evidence, and never visited or talked to hunt supporters. 'It was a very sad reflection on our democratic process,' says Hoey. 'If politicians behaved like this with hunting, you wonder what other issues could suffer in a similar way. People outside Parliament should be concerned about the ignorance of many MPs.'

We should also be concerned about the way in which anti-hunting groups were able to infiltrate the grassroots of the Labour Party. Over the years, the League Against Cruel Sports and other anti-hunting organisations provided significant finance to the Labour Party and its local constituency parties. They did so not to promote socialism but their own agenda. In return, many MPs who knew little or nothing about hunting agreed to vote for a ban. One Labour MP admitted to Richard Jarman, then a Labour councillor in London and later Head of Communications at the Country Land and Business Association (CLA): 'I know that we should have gone down the route of licensed hunting, rather than an outright ban, but most of us had promised we'd vote for a ban and we had to deliver.' Powerful and aggressive lobbying, backed by cash, clearly influenced the way in which some politicians voted.

If there is one document which you might reasonably expect MPs to have read before voting on hunting legislation, it would be the Burns Report. Lord Burns and his committee were asked to explore the practical aspects of different sorts of hunting and their impact on the rural economy, agriculture, the social and cultural life of the countryside and the management of wildlife. The committee was also asked to speculate on what would happen were hunting to be banned. But how reliable was the evidence presented to Burns, and later to the Portcullis Hearings? Who was to be trusted, and who was not?

The second chapter – 'Corrupting the Evidence' – examines the way in which scientists and lobbying groups have misused science to further their political aims. This has been most clearly, and publicly, illustrated by conflicting research studies investigating the shooting and wounding of foxes. This is of more than academic interest, as the Hunting Act is founded on the supposition that shooting causes less suffering than hunting. I argue that Professor Stephen Harris, whose work has been widely used by anti-hunting organisations and MPs, has presented evidence on shooting and wounding which is profoundly flawed. 'Science cannot make decisions for us,' suggests Peter Luff, Conservative MP for Mid-Worcestershire and one of the founders of the All Party Parliamentary Middle Way Group, 'but science can inform and it can guide.' Which is why it is important that scientists conduct their research in as objective a manner as possible, and ensure that their prejudices fit the facts, rather than the other way round.

Over the years, the organisations responsible for promoting and overseeing hunting of various sorts – from hunting with hounds to chasing rabbits with lurchers and using terriers to dig out foxes – have periodically made claims which simply do not bear examination. The same can be said for the League Against Cruel Sports. None of this should come as a surprise. These organisations, whether pro- or anti-hunting, will inevitably muster whatever arguments they can to justify their cause. Scrupulous honesty and good propaganda make poor bedfellows.

When we listen to the pro-hunting lobby and the League we know we should be on our guard. But the RSPCA is an altogether different beast. Its patron is Her Majesty the Queen, which suggests a high degree of respectability. We all know that RSPCA inspectors do a wonderful job rescuing maltreated cats and dogs, providing them with homes and prosecuting brutish people who neglect or persecute animals. And over the years, the RSPCA has called on the expertise of respected scientists to champion important reforms in factory farming, the export of live animals and vivisection. We have grown to trust the RSPCA as an organisation committed to improving animal welfare.

That trust, I suggest in the third chapter – 'Lobbyists or Liars?' – is no longer fully deserved. During the course of the last few years the RSPCA has fed dubious information to MPs and ignored its obligation to provide clear evidence for the claims it has made on the issue of hunting and cruelty. These obligations are legal as well as moral for a charity like the RSPCA. However, in its zeal to get hunting banned, the RSPCA has chosen to ignore compelling evidence which suggests that shooting foxes is likely to cause high levels of wounding, and therefore suffering. The RSPCA's director-general, Jackie Ballard, has even called into question the notion of suffering. In response to a letter from Lembit Öpik, Liberal Democrat MP for Montgomeryshire and co-founder of the Middle Way Group, she wrote: 'As you will be aware it is impossible to prove, absolutely, suffering in another living thing, even in another human. There is not absolute proof that wounded foxes suffer'[3]. Does this mean we are now free to kick the cat in a fit of pique?

The final chapter – 'Searching for Solutions' – explores a legislative approach which would go a long way towards improving the welfare of all wild mammals. This approach has been promoted by the All Party Parliamentary Middle Way Group, and it has received wide support from many countryside organisations, as well as in the House of Lords. It involves a licensing system for hunting with dogs and a new Bill which will make it an offence intentionally to cause undue suffering to any wild mammal. The legislation will be based on science rather than sentimentality, and it will establish benchmarks for animal welfare and best practice which can be accurately measured and enforced.

This essay has been commissioned by the All Party Parliamentary Middle Way Group, and in many ways – though not all – it reflects the Middle Way Group's views and beliefs. MPs, scientists and animal welfare organisations that take exception to *Rural Rites* may therefore be tempted to dismiss its thesis on the grounds that I am not an objective observer, but a hired hand. I would contend that I am both.

I have never been an active participant in any form of hunting, and before I researched the subject in detail I possessed no strong opinions about whether it was a good or bad thing. Had anybody asked me during the 1970s and 1980s whether I would support a ban on hunting, I would have said 'no' for the simple reason that I am instinctively opposed to outlawing anything unless it is demonstrably harmful. In the early 1990s it was obvious that a Labour government would soon get back into power, and that legislation to ban hunting would have a real chance of success. I decided to make a radio programme for the BBC World Service, exploring the pros and cons of fox-hunting. I did my best to be impartial. I went out with two hunts – a shire pack in Dorset with well-to-do riders and a foot pack in Yorkshire with a working-class following – and I spent time with hunt saboteurs, farmers, landowners and representatives of organisations promoting and opposing a ban.

Soon after Labour won the 1997 General Election, Michael Foster, Labour MP for Worcester, introduced a Private Member's Bill to ban hunting with dogs. Hunting was now officially on the political agenda. I made another programme for the BBC World Service, concentrating this time on the influence of hunting on rural life. Fox-hunting, I now realised, was about far more than the chasing and killing of foxes. It provided work for some and entertainment for others; in some places, though by no means everywhere, it served as a reasonably efficient form of pest control and wildlife management.

Had the debate about hunting remained bipartisan, as it had been in the past, with one side arguing in favour of a ban, and another against, I doubt whether I would have continued to take a journalistic interest in the subject. But a simple act of apostasy by Jim Barrington changed the entire nature of the debate. Barrington, executive director of the League Against Cruel Sports, began to question whether a hunting ban was in the best interests of the fox. He had come to believe that a straightforward ban of the sort championed by the League could lead to more foxes dying, often more horribly than was already the case. At the same time, he still had serious misgivings about certain hunting practices, such as the digging out of foxes with terriers. Was there, he wondered, a compromise solution? To find out, he opened up a dialogue with hunters, and as a result he was forced from the League.

I first met Barrington in January 1997 when I attended a meeting held in the Wiltshire farmhouse of Roger Scruton, the fox-hunting philosopher. During the course of a lengthy dinner, Barrington and a group of like-minded colleagues debated hunting reforms with Scruton, Captain Ian Farquhar, joint-master of the Duke of Beaufort's Foxhounds, and Lord Mancroft, vice-chairman of the British Field Sports Society. I wrote about this remarkable meeting, at which the hunters suggested they could live with the idea of some form of licensed and regulated hunting, in an article for the *Daily Telegraph*.[4] Inevitably, there were some cries of protest from hunting people who were still naive enough, or arrogant enough, to think the status quo, based on self-regulation, could prevail. The League reacted to news of the meeting with uncharacteristic silence, although it continued to denigrate Barrington in its in-house publication, *Wildlife Guardian*.

Following the meeting, I suggested to Barrington that I should write an impartial analysis of fox-hunting, in which I would explore the nature of the activity and describe the sort of proposals which his newly formed group, Wildlife Network, were promoting – with the proviso that I would draw my own conclusions about whether they made sense. During the course of the summer of 1997, I researched and wrote *Fox-Hunting: Beyond the Propaganda*, which was published by Wildlife Network.[5] The booklet was launched in Westminster with the help of the Conservative MP Peter Luff, who was then chairman of the Agriculture Select Committee.

Soon afterwards, Foster's Private Member's Bill had its second reading. Kate Hoey displayed a copy of the booklet to her Labour colleagues, who were much put out to discover she was opposed to the Bill. 'I welcome very much the booklet produced by the Wildlife Network,' she told the chamber. 'That document should be read by everyone. It talks about getting rid of some of the abuses, such as terrier hunting and other practices, that I find distasteful... That is the way forward: it is not through legislation and banning.'

Hoey's belief that hunting should come under some form of

regulation, rather than be the subject of a ban, struck a chord with several other MPs, including Peter Luff, Lembit Öpik and Llin Golding. They decided to establish an all party group to promote licensed hunting, and invited Jim Barrington to act as its secretary. Within a short period of time, the Middle Way Group became a force to be reckoned with.

This brings me back to the issue of impartiality. Insofar as I have taken sides in the hunting debate, it has been with the Middle Way Group rather than any of the factions promoting or opposing a ban. I have done so not because the Middle Way Group has paid me to write this essay, but because I believe that the Middle Way Group has come up with credible and fair proposals for legislation which, if implemented, would improve animal welfare in the countryside without unduly compromising our civil liberties.

CHAPTER I

Outlawing Your Enemies

In 1995, just over a hundred years after Parliament first debated banning hunting with dogs, the Labour Party pledged in a policy document that it would make time available for a free vote on the abolition of fox-hunting, deer-hunting and hare-coursing with dogs. Curiously, *A Working Countryside* made no mention of hare-hunting, which suggests the authors were unaware of its existence. Soon after Labour came to power, Michael Foster introduced a Private Member's Bill to ban hunting. The Wild Mammals (Hunting with Dogs) Bill received its second reading on 28 November 1997. 411 MPs voted for a ban; 151 voted against. However, the Bill ran out of parliamentary time and failed to become law.

During the coming years, further attempts were made to resolve the hunting issue. Jack Straw, Labour MP for Blackburn and Home Secretary, asked Lord Burns to conduct an inquiry into the impacts and significance of hunting with dogs. This helped to shape Straw's thinking on the subject. He favoured a compromise solution which would have allowed hunting to continue under licence and subject to certain conditions (as did Lord Burns, although he did not make his view explicit till later), and he introduced an 'Options Bill' during the 2000/01 session. MPs were given the opportunity to vote for one of three measures: a ban, the status quo or regulation. MPs voted 373–158 in favour of a ban. When the Bill went to the House of Lords, peers voted for the status quo. Once again, the bill ran out of time.

Labour's 2001 manifesto vowed that Parliament would be given time 'to reach a conclusion on this issue'. Responsibility for hunting matters shifted from the Home Office to the Department for Environment, Food and Rural Affairs (DEFRA), and the person charged with sorting out the hunting issue was Alun Michael, Labour MP for Cardiff South and Penarth and Minister for Rural Affairs. In 2002, a 'vote of intention' found that MPs, if offered a choice of a ban, the status quo or regulation – the Middle Way option, as it was now known – would again vote overwhelmingly for a ban. The Lords, in contrast, shifted away from their previous position in favour of the status quo to vote by a convincing margin for the Middle Way option.

Alun Michael then established a six-month period of public consultations, which culminated in September 2002 with three days of hearings, organised by DEFRA and chaired by the minister, at Portcullis House in Westminster. The hearings were followed by the publication of the Government's second Hunting Bill, whose contents were based on the minister's weighing up of the evidence presented during the consultation process and at the hearings. The Alun Michael Bill, as it was known, began as a regulatory bill, but during the committee stage anti-hunting MPs changed it to such an extent that it would have been almost impossible for hunts to pass the stringent licensing requirements. When the legislation received its third reading in the House of Commons in the summer of 2003, an amendment introduced by Tony Banks turned it into a banning bill. It now became known as the Banks Bill. The Bill was sent to the House of Lords at the end of July, but the parliamentary session was drawing to an end and the Lords were given insufficient time to debate the Bill, so it ran out of time.

The Government's third Hunting Bill – the Banks Bill – was first debated in the House of Commons on 15 September 2004. A torrid session of parliamentary ping-pong saw the Bill bounce backwards and forwards between the Commons and the Lords. The Commons sent the Lords the banning Bill. The Lords returned the Bill in the form originally drafted by Alun Michael. Although the Prime

Minister, the Foreign Secretary and other prominent members of the Cabinet voted for an amendment which would have reintroduced a regulatory process similar to the one proposed by Alun Michael, the vast majority of Labour MPs, most urban-based Liberal Democrats and a few Conservatives voted against the amendment. The Speaker invoked the seldom-used Parliament Act to assert the will of the Commons over the Lords. The Banks Bill became law.

The Hunting Act was ostensibly about animal welfare, but for many MPs animal welfare was a Trojan horse. What they really wanted to do was prevent a tiresome minority, the majority of whom were probably rural Tories, from enjoying their traditional pastimes – or 'blood sports' as they liked to describe them. Some MPs have been perfectly candid about this. 'There is not a subject under the sun that is better suited to us for raising our morale in the constituencies than a ban on fox-hunting,' Dennis Skinner, Labour MP for Bolsover, told the House of Commons on 17 June 2004. It raised morale because it provided Labour MPs and their supporters with a means of getting their own back for the political defeats they suffered during the Thatcher era. 'This has nothing to do with animal welfare – this is for the miners,' Skinner told Jim Barrington at the Labour Party conference later that year. In short, the hunting ban was an act of retribution. 'The people marching today', Gerald Kaufman told Jonathan Dimbleby in September 2002, when reflecting on a pro-hunting demonstration, 'didn't march for the miners when thousands of their jobs were taken away by Thatcher.' Now they would be made to suffer for their failure to support Arthur Scargill and his trade union.

One of the most overt admissions that the ban on hunting was about more than animal welfare came from Peter Bradley, Labour MP for The Wrekin and parliamentary secretary to Alun Michael. In an article in the *Sunday Telegraph*, published the weekend after the Hunting Act was passed, he wrote: 'We ought at last to own up to it: the struggle over the bill was not just about animal welfare and personal freedom, it was class war.' Curiously, Bradley went on to argue that it was not traditional class warfare, with the tribunes rising up against the toffs; rather, it was the other way round. It is hard to work out precisely what Bradley was claiming, so intellectually inchoate is his argument, but he clearly saw the Bill as a good way of attacking 'the privileged minority which for centuries ran this country from the manor houses of Rural England'. He did not seem to realise that the class profile of people who hunt – and here I include people who hunt with lurchers and whippets and terriers as well as the traditional mounted packs – is much the same as the class profile of the country as a whole.

Talk to the handful of Labour MPs who voted against the ban and they will confirm that, for many of their colleagues, animal welfare was the least of their concerns. 'A few justified a ban on animal welfare grounds without understanding the issue,' says Kate Hoey. 'Most just had a romanticised idea of fluffy little foxes being chased by horrible people on horses in red coats.' This view is confirmed by Lord Donoughue, who was Minister for Farming and the Food Industry from 1997 to 1999. 'I've spent 40 years fighting political zealots in the Labour Party and I recognise certain familiar characteristics among those who wish to ban hunting,' he says. 'They don't care about welfare or cruelty. They just dislike certain people. They are guided by ignorance and prejudice.'

This helps to explain why the quality of debate was often so poor. Many of those who favoured a ban couched their opposition to hunting in highly emotional language – there was much talk of a barbaric minority, of foxes being savagely ripped apart – and they clearly knew little about the countryside. As Lembit Öpik puts it: 'Basil Brush had much more impact than Bertrand Russell on the philosophical quality of debate on the pro-ban side.' According to Öpik, many pro-ban MPs wilfully ignored the evidence, sometimes to the point of deluding themselves into believing that the evidence did not exist.

Take, for example, the issue of fox-hunting and pest control. It is true that in the past the hunting lobby has exaggerated the role which hunting plays in controlling foxes. The fact is that in some areas, such as the Welsh uplands, hunting with dogs is an important form of pest control; in other areas, it serves no such function. However, Martin Salter, Labour MP for Reading West, and the party's spokesman on shooting, was among the pro-banners who claimed that fox-hunting played no role whatsoever in pest control. Anyone who had read the Burns Report, or spent any time talking to farmers in the British uplands, would know this was nonsense. Like many of his colleagues, Salter simply hadn't bothered to do his homework, or his fieldwork.

In the corridors and bars of Westminster there was much triumphalism when the Hunting Act became law. After all, this had been a long struggle spanning generations. But not all those who voted for the ban took pleasure in the new law. 'Many of them were plainly embarrassed,' says Lord Mancroft. 'They secretly knew the ban was ridiculous, and were just a little bit ashamed of themselves.' One might have expected MPs who voted for the ban to be magnanimous in victory. Not all of them were. Immediately after the vote, Lembit Öpik suggested that he and Jim Barrington should go down to Strangers Bar, a popular Westminster watering hole. On the way in, Barrington bumped into Jim Dowd, Labour MP for Lewisham West. Dowd had previously told Barrington, when they met one day in the gents, that the people of inner-city Lewisham had elected him to ban hunting – clearly a ludicrous claim.

'By the way, Jim,' said Barrington as he entered the bar, 'I'm sure the people of Lewisham will be delighted to know you voted to increase animal suffering.'

'Barrington, I always thought you were a c∗∗∗' replied Dowd, 'Come outside and I'll smack you in the mouth.'

This was a crude but accurate reflection of the debating strategy favoured by some pro-ban MPs when away from the chamber, as Peter Luff, the leading Conservative in the Middle Way Group, discovered when he confronted Martin Salter. Salter had been distributing a leaflet inside the chamber which apparently drew a parallel between pro-hunting groups and the extreme right British National Party. When Luff asked for a copy in the Members' lobby, he was rebuffed. He told Salter his behaviour was disgraceful. Salter responded by saying: 'Say that again and I'll break every f***ing bone in your f***ing body.' This threat, which would have constituted an offence outside Parliament, was reported to the Sergeant-at-Arms.

Another splendid illustration of the anti-hunting yobbish tendency was provided more recently by Paul Flynn, Labour MP for Newport West. The Middle Way Group sent him, and many other MPs, a copy of an article from the magazine *Country Illustrated* which discussed, among other things, the remarkable claim made by the RSPCA's director-general that there is no absolute proof that wounded foxes suffer. Flynn replied in the following terms: 'Vacuous, brain-dead and stupid. This is the most futile e-mail I've had this year. Are you brain-damaged?'

A great many MPs who voted for a ban would be hard pressed to construct a logical argument against hunting. They seldom listened to the debates; they certainly never read the Burns Report or the transcripts of the Portcullis House hearings. It would be preposterous to suggest that this significant body of men and women were all consumed with class hatred, or violently opposed to people who wander around the countryside with cloth caps, tweedy jackets and red coats. So why did they vote for a ban? The answer for many is that they and their constituency parties had committed themselves to a ban, often many years ago, sometimes in return for financial support from organisations like the League Against Cruel Sports.

Lord Donoughue tells a story about a Labour colleague which is indicative, in his view, of the way in which animal rights organisations bought influence within the Labour Party. After his colleague's constituency party had conducted interviews for a new parliamentary candidate, the committee chairman said they would choose him – providing he accepted certain undertakings. 'The only one he could remember', recalls Lord Donoughue, 'was that he had to vote for a ban on hunting, whatever his views. He said this was an obligation the constituency party had accepted when one of the animal rights organisations had given money.' In short, they took cash in return for favours. Lord Donoughue's colleague agreed to vote for a hunting ban whenever the opportunity arose, not because he believed in a ban, but because he wanted the seat.

In correspondence with Peter Luff in 2001, the League Against Cruel Sports' chief executive, Douglas Batchelor, wrote: 'The League has not funded the campaign of any MP, pro or anti-hunting. All that our members have done is to offer help to MPs who have wanted it.' Bachelor ignores, or was unaware of, the significant contributions made to the Labour Party by the League, dating back to the late 1970s. In fact, the League played a wonderfully astute long game. During the 1980s, when Labour seemed unelectable, the League was a generous ally and supporter.

In 1979, shortly before that year's general election, the League gave the Labour Party £80,000, £50,000 of which was to go towards the party's general funds and £30,000 to promote animal welfare. Two Conservative members of the League objected and the matter was subject to legal action. The courts decided that it was quite legitimate for the League to give £30,000 to promote animal welfare, a euphemism for promoting a ban on hunting. However, the Labour Party should not have accepted £50,000 for general funds from the League. It was obliged to return it, with interest. Richard Course, who was then director, returned most of the money to the Labour Party by giving sums of £200 or less to large numbers of constituency parties for the next general election, thus remaining within the letter of the law.

This policy of providing what seemed like relatively small donations continued during the 1980s. For example, shortly before the election of 1987, on 15 May, the League gave 75 Labour constituency parties sums ranging from £50 to £200 for the purposes of 'political promotion'. This simply meant that most MPs would add a line or two to their campaign literature saying they would support a ban on hunting. Of the 75 MPs whose campaigns benefited from these donations, only two were to oppose a hunting ban in the future: Kate Hoey and Jeff Rooker, then MP for Birmingham Perry Barr. The rest, including Alun Michael, Tony Benn, Anne Clwyd, Neil Kinnock, Michael Meacher, Peter Hain, Kevin McNamara, Eric Heffer, Paul Flynn and Jim Dowd, have consistently voted for a ban, although Alun Michael could argue that he suppressed his urge for a complete ban when he introduced a regulatory bill.

From the point of view of the anti-hunting movement, money given to the Labour Party was money well spent. Assiduous lobbying and frequent donations were helping to secure votes for a ban. One day, Labour would get back into power and a ban would be delivered. No doubt the Political Animal Lobby's decision to give £1 million to the Labour Party prior to the 1997 general election was a further inducement to the party to deal once and for all with this issue; and to MPs not to waver in their commitment to a ban.[1]

During the days before the final passage of the Hunting Act, many Labour MPs approached Kate Hoey and told her: 'It's ridiculous, it's taking up all this time, and I don't really care about it, but I said I'd vote against hunting, so I'd better carry on with it.' What depresses Hoey is that if something like this can happen with hunting, it could happen on other issues which are far more important. Of course, voting for a ban was seen by many MPs to play well with the electorate. As Michael Foster pointed out after MPs voted overwhelmingly in favour of his private member's bill in 1997, Parliament was simply echoing the will of the people: at the time over 70 per cent of those canvassed in national opinion polls supported a ban on hunting. However, support for a total ban gradually began to wane, which suggests that the public was taking greater notice of the evidence than many MPs. In an opinion poll conducted in 2004, 59 per cent of those polled were opposed to a complete ban, with a majority of these favouring the sort of regulatory approach advocated by the Middle Way Group.

Judging from his pronouncements during the early years of his premiership, Tony Blair also thought support for a ban played well with the public, as well as with his own backbenchers and his wife. On 30 September 1999, he told Radio 4: 'I am opposed to hunting.' On 17 January 2001, during Prime Minister's Question Time, he said: 'I have made it quite clear, and my position has not changed. I am opposed to fox-hunting for the reasons that I have given on many occasions.' When asked for his views on BBC's *Question Time* in 1999, the Prime Minister declared: 'We had one try at it last session – people like myself voted in favour of banning fox-hunting. I voted for it.' This was untrue. He had not voted at all. Again, on *Question Time* on 30 May 2001, he claimed, 'I happened to vote in favour of a ban.' He was referring to Jack Straw's Options Bill, and he was dissembling again. He did not vote. The Prime Minister also claimed that Michael Foster's Bill failed because it was blocked by the House of Lords. This was also untrue. It failed because the Government refused to allow the Bill more parliamentary time and it never reached the Lords.

When Tony Blair went to see Lord Jenkins of Hillhead shortly before the latter's death, the conversation turned to hunting. Lord Jenkins later told friends that the Prime Minister had said: 'Roy, I wish I had never heard the word hunting. We are in such a mess. I do not know how we are going to get out of it.'[2] The Prime Minister did belatedly try to get out of the mess when the Banks Bill returned to the Commons for the last time on 18 November 2004. He backed an amendment tabled by Huw Irranca-Davies, the Labour MP for Ogmore, which would have overturned the outright ban on hunting and reintroduced a licensing system similar to the one in the original Alun Michael Bill. Many people in the hunting world believed this was a cynical ploy to curry favour with the countryside. This may be unfair.

'I think the Government did genuinely listen in the end,' says Baroness Golding. When the chairs of the Middle Way Group – Baroness Golding, Lembit Öpik and Peter Luff – visited Tony

Blair to air their concerns, they told him that if hunting with dogs were banned, animal rights groups and some MPs would begin to agitate for bans on shooting and fishing. 'He was quite shocked by that,' recalls Baroness Golding. According to Huw Irranca-Davies, the Prime Minister's decision to favour regulation had nothing to do with political posturing. 'I believe he came to the rational conclusion that this was the way forward,' says Irranca-Davies. 'My regret is that that position was reached by him too late in the day. If he had come to that position and made it clear many months before, there would have been time for other people to look at it once again and fall in line behind the Prime Minister.'

When Tony Blair eventually writes his memoirs, he will recall his role in the hunting saga with a shudder of regret. Initially, he played to the gallery and lied about his voting behaviour, presumably to garner popularity with the public and his party. In the end, he allowed Tony Banks and his allies to hijack a Government Bill – had he wished, he could simply have dropped it – and he must now live with Lord Jenkins' admonition ringing in his ears. 'Tony,' he told him, 'if you invoke the Parliament Act it will be the most illiberal act of the last century.'

It is hard not to feel some sympathy for Alun Michael, whose efforts to resolve the hunting issue eventually came to nothing. Opinions about whether he was the right man to do the job vary. Some thought him an unsuitable choice as he had frequently voted for a hunting ban in the past. 'Blair told Michael to try and find a compromise solution,' says Lord Donoughue, 'but he made a mistake appointing someone who'd always been committed to a ban.' In Kate Hoey's view, Michael should have made his beliefs plain to the Prime Minister and refused to accept the job of drafting hunting legislation. Lord Mancroft is not so sure. 'I think he really wanted to do the right thing,' he says. 'The problem was that he was attempting to do something which was undoable.' Over dinner in the House of Lords, Michael told Lord Mancroft that he thought he could come up with a compromise solution which involved some hunting under licence, and that he could sell the idea to Labour backbenchers. 'I said I didn't think he could; that the backbenches would trash a licensing bill,' recalls Lord Mancroft. 'That's exactly what happened.'

From the outset Michael made it clear that one of his aims was to look for common ground 'wherever possible'.[3] Hunting would be allowed to continue where it was necessary, and where it could be established that it was the least cruel method of control: hence his two defining 'principles' of utility and least suffering. He let it be known that he was approaching the subject with an open mind and that his draft legislation would be based on hard evidence rather than sentiment. However, there is plenty of evidence to suggest that the Minister for Rural Affairs favoured the pro-ban lobby and accepted its evidence, however suspect, more readily than that of the hunting lobby or the Middle Way Group.

Look, for example, at the way in which the Portcullis House hearings were constituted. During the preparatory period, Alun Michael went out of his way to appease the Campaign for the Protection of Hunted Animals, an anti-hunting coalition of the RSPCA, the League Against Cruel Sports and the International Fund for Animal Welfare (IFAW).[4] These organisations, collectively and individually, made it quite clear that they thought the hearings unnecessary, just as they had made plain their opposition to the Burns Inquiry and the six-month period of public consultations which preceded the hearings. Michael realised that the success of the hearings depended on all sides giving evidence, and to keep the Campaign for the Protection of Hunted Animals on board he was prepared to let them dictate the rules of engagement. He was also frequently seen fraternising with them after sessions.

The Countryside Alliance and the Middle Way Group took the view that each party should choose its own witnesses. If the Alliance or the Campaign for the Protection of Hunted Animals decided to call, say, Saddam Hussein or Brigitte Bardot, then that was their business. However, Michael told the Middle Way Group that the

Campaign for the Protection of Hunted Animals threatened to withdraw from the entire proceedings if the Middle Way Group was allowed to call Professor Stuart Harrop. A former RSPCA employee and now Professor of Wildlife Management Law at Kent University, Harrop's animal welfare credentials were impeccable and he would have been a particularly persuasive witness in favour of licensed hunting. The Middle Way Group reluctantly agreed to give way, providing the minister agreed to see Harrop privately. He did agree, but the meeting never took place.

Just as galling, as far as the Middle Way Group was concerned, was the fact that Michael, having initially insisted that the evidence presented at the hearings should be science-based, allowed the Campaign for the Protection of Hunted Animals to call as one of its witnesses Reverend Professor Andrew Linzey, a theologian from Oxford University who told the hearings that hunting 'belongs to that class of always morally impermissible acts along with rape, child abuse and torture'. That the minister was prepared to accept such a gratuitously offensive contribution to hearings which were supposed to be dealing with science and hard facts was astonishing. Presumably, he felt that was the price he had to pay to keep the Campaign for the Protection of Hunted Animals involved.

The anti-hunting organisations must also have been gratified by the way in which Alun Michael frequently sifted evidence in their favour. This was particularly obvious when it came to his attitude towards deer-hunting. I can understand somebody disliking the activity – the sight of a stag held at bay after a long chase is unedifying to many. But Michael had promised to base his decisions on the available evidence. In this case, he failed to do so.

In a statement to the House of Commons on 3 December 2002, he said: 'I have spent time there [Exmoor] and met all the groups to understand the reasoning behind their defence of hunting. The evidence is conclusive and that is why I believe it must be banned.' In the same statement he claimed: 'Incontrovertible evidence shows that the activities of hare-coursing and deer hunting cannot meet the two tests [utility and least suffering], so these activities will be banned.' During the Second Reading of his Hunting Bill, the minister was asked to justify his claim that the evidence was incontrovertible. He replied as follows: 'It is necessary to control deer numbers and to disperse the herd to protect crops and growing trees. Although the test of utility may be passed, the test of cruelty – to inflict the least suffering – has not. Both the Bateson Report and subsequent evidence to Burns showed clear evidence of chased deer suffering even if they are not caught.'

In an exchange of emails between Professor Bateson and one of his critics, the former wrote: 'Only someone who was scientifically illiterate could argue that evidence from a new area of research was "incontrovertible"'. This is precisely what the minister had done.[5] Michael's contention that 'evidence to Burns showed clear evidence of chased deer suffering even if they are not caught' may be true, but Michael failed to reveal that the evidence was not unreservedly endorsed by Burns and his colleagues. The Burns Report states: 'There is also a lack of firm information about what happens to deer which escape, although the available research suggests they are likely to recover.'

In fact, Michael was highly selective in his reading of the Burns Report. He used the following quote from the report to justify his decision to introduce a complete ban on deer-hunting: 'Stalking, if carried out to a high standard and with the availability of a dog or dogs to find any wounded deer that escape, is in principle the best method of culling deer from an animal welfare perspective. In particular, it obviates the need to chase deer in the way which occurs in hunting.'

However, the minister failed to quote the preceding and following paragraphs in the Burns Report. The preceding paragraph states: 'It is clear that more work would be required in order to provide further scientific evidence about the welfare of hunted deer and how hunting compares with stalking.' In other words, we do not have proof that hunting causes more suffering than shooting, as

Michael implied. The paragraph which followed the excerpt used by the minister is even more relevant, as it helps to define Burns' qualifying phrase 'in principle'. It reads: 'A great deal depends, however, on the skill and care taken by the stalker. It is unfortunate that there is no reliable information on wounding rates... In the event of a ban on hunting there is a risk that a greater number of deer than at present would be shot by less skilful shooters, in which case wounding rates would increase.' In other words, a ban on hunting could lead to more shooting and this, in turn, could lead to greater suffering, not less. A hunted animal, after all, either dies or gets away; an animal which is shot and wounded could suffer for days or weeks. Indeed, as we shall see later, the ban on hunting on National Trust properties, introduced in 1997, had already led to a significant increase in the suffering of deer on Exmoor.

Alun Michael based his legislation on two 'principles': utility and least suffering. These principles were to provide the basis of the two tests that hunting would have to satisfy if it were to be allowed by the Registrar, an individual who would be appointed by Government to oversee the licensing process.[6] Applicants would have to show, first, that the hunting they proposed to do was necessary for pest-control purposes; and second, that hunting was the method of control which involved the least suffering.

One of the defects of this whole process was that the various participants in the hunting consultations and the hearings, as well as MPs and members of the House of Lords, were obliged to accept Michael's principles. There were no public – or private, as far as one can tell – consultations about the principles themselves. They were written in stone. But did they make sense?

Principles, by definition, must be universally applicable. You cannot have principles which apply to one activity that involves the use of wildlife – say, hunting with dogs – but not to another; to angling, for example, or shooting pheasants, or the commercial harvesting of mackerel. As the Game Conservancy Trust pointed out, any acceptable criteria for hunting with dogs should apply to shooting and fishing, as well as to pest control and commercial harvesting. But this was never the intention. The principles, in short, were not true principles.

Even had they been, they were ill-chosen. Take, first, the principle of utility. Who should decide exactly what is useful, or necessary, and what is not? For a vegetarian, the rearing of sheep and poultry is not necessary, and neither, therefore, is the control of foxes and other predators. For the farmer, in contrast, the rearing of livestock provides a livelihood, and anything which endangers his animals threatens him and his family. The killing of foxes is therefore necessary.

Michael himself was clearly confused about how to define his principle of utility. In an explanatory letter outlining his plans, sent on 10 April 2002, he wrote: '"Utility" addresses the need for particular activities, particularly in the work of land and wildlife managers. It might be described as the need of usefulness of an activity for vermin control, wildlife management, habitat protection or land management and conservation.' Translated into plain English, this suggests that Michael accepted that hunting had a range of functions which could be considered useful. He still held this view in November 2002, long after the Portcullis House hearings, but he had jettisoned it by the time he published his Bill in December. The principle of utility had been narrowed to just one activity: pest control. Hunts would no longer be able to claim that they served any other useful purpose, such as habitat conservation, despite the fact that the area of woodlands managed by fox hunts was roughly double the entire woodland area within national nature reserves in England and Wales.[7]

As the Game Conservancy Trust pointed out in one of its submissions, the proof of utility and necessity would be a technically demanding exercise.[8] Its research showed that within England and Wales every aspect of fox control, from the perceived need for control, to preferred methods of culling and population density, varied on a regional basis. The Registrar responsible for assessing whether hunting satisfied the test of utility would be faced with an enormously difficult task, because hunting's utility, even in terms of pest control, would vary from one area to another.

Assessing the second principle would be even more difficult. We simply do not have sufficient scientific evidence to establish which method of control causes the least, or the most suffering. The Registrar, had the Alun Michael Bill become law, would often have to make decisions on the basis of his or her own perceptions, and would be guided by gut-feeling rather than hard science. Is hunting more cruel than shooting? The answer is sometimes yes, and sometimes no. Again, as the Game Conservancy points out, 'Very rarely does any single culling method excel in all aspects, and often there are trade-offs between effectiveness, target-specificity, operating efficiency and humaneness.

Looking back, it is hard to see what purpose the Portcullis House hearings served. They allowed three different constituencies – the Campaign for the Protection of Hunted Animals, the Countryside Alliance and the Middle Way Group – to present their evidence through chosen witnesses, and sometimes to air their prejudices. But they did not come to any firm conclusions, as the Burns Inquiry had, and as public inquiries into planning issues invariably do. There was no summary to guide MPs, as there was with the Burns Report, and if MPs chose not to read the copious documentation from the hearings it was hardly surprising. In fact, the hearings had about them the whiff of a show trial. On their conclusion, Michael could claim that he had given everyone a fair hearing, that justice had been done, regardless of whether or not it had been. As it happens, most pro-ban MPs were not remotely interested in the evidence presented here or anywhere else: they had already decided they wanted a total ban. In the end, nobody got what they wanted. The minister was vanquished by his own backbenchers, and the ban turned out to be, well, not really a ban at all.

If the House of Commons were a person, he would be cringing with embarrassment and hoping friends and colleagues would have the decency not to mention the Hunting Act, much as a middle-aged man who has made a clumsy pass at a young secretary at the office party hopes no one will later remind him, or his wife, of his infelicity. Since the Act came into force, the hard core of MPs who pushed for a ban has been remarkably silent on the subject. You can understand why. The Hunting Act diminished the standing of Parliament in the eyes of many. It may have cost some their seats. Hunting has carried on in one way or another; not a single organised hunt has disbanded; and the hunts have made fools of the law.

There is no doubt that the passage of the Hunting Act did considerable damage to the reputation of Parliament, and especially to the House of Commons. 'This country risks being governed on the basis of emotion, rather than fact,' suggests Lembit Öpik. 'As politicians, we are paid a lot of money to do the right thing – not to say: "I've made up my mind; don't confuse me with the facts"'. But this was the attitude of a great many MPs. They were much less willing to look at the facts than members of the House of Lords. 'If you read Hansard,' suggests Lord Livsey, a sheep farmer and former Liberal Democrat MP for a mid-Wales constituency, 'you will see there are an enormous number of quotations from the Lords referring to the Burns Report and other evidence. Many MPs, on the other hand, simply ignored the evidence. It may sound trite, but they pursued their prejudices in a very single-minded way, and they chose to ignore the impact of the ban on the welfare of the fox, which I find extraordinary.'

There was certainly a backlash to the Hunting Act at the 2005 General Election. A campaign organised by Vote-OK encouraged between 7,000 and 10,000 hunt supporters to provide help to pro-hunting candidates who lay a close second to anti-hunting MPs in 127 marginal seats, and to around a dozen pro-hunting MPs who had small majorities and were at risk of losing their seats to anti-hunting candidates. Over 3 million leaflets were delivered, 2 million envelopes hand-addressed and 55,000 posters erected. 'We were not banging the drum about hunting,' explains Charles

Mann, Vote-OK's national campaign director, 'we were simply lending greater firepower to candidates who were supportive of hunting, entirely on their terms.' Twenty-nine anti-hunting MPs lost their seats, and according to Mann, 19 new pro-hunting MPs said they would never have gained their seats without the help of Vote-OK.

Immediately after the Act came into force, in February 2005, Roger Scruton gathered together a motley collection of dogs on his Wiltshire farm and set out on a mouse hunt. First they drew a covert in the kitchen. Failing to find a mouse, they then set off across the fields. 'All trails led to nothing,' recalls Scruton, 'and we failed to kill a mouse.' Scruton phoned the local police and told them that he thought he had just committed an offence under the Hunting Act. He was given a crime number, but the police took no further action.

Before the ban came into force Scruton had helped to draft the Hunting Declaration, which committed its signatories – some 45,000 – to breaking any law which sought to ban hunting. 'But the law is so unclear, we are not even sure how to break it,' he says. By going out on a mouse hunt, Scruton was making a serious point about the inept drafting of the Act, with its numerous anomalies. For example, you can hunt a rat or a rabbit with dogs, but not a mouse; you can use a terrier to flush a fox from its den providing you are protecting birds that you later intend to shoot, but not to protect birds that you don't intend to shoot, or lambs or wildlife.

Before the Act was passed, several senior police officers voiced their concerns about the draft Hunting Bill. 'I do not have any dedicated resources to police hunts,' said Maria Wallis, the Chief Constable of Devon and Cornwall, in February 2004.[9] 'Resources have to come from elsewhere. I'm concerned that a hunting ban could cause difficulties.' Chief Inspector Jan Berry, chair of the Police Federation, expressed similar misgivings when interviewed on BBC Radio 4's *Any Questions*.[10] 'Our duty as police officers is to try and enforce the law without fear or favour and that does become increasingly difficult when a law is particularly unfavourable,' she said. 'It will be extremely difficult to police and it will be extremely resource-intensive.' Privately, many police officers have been even more scathing. 'If you talk to the local police in my constituency about the Hunting Act, they just smile and nod,' says Peter Luff. 'They know the law is mad. Many of them hunt or shoot themselves, and they don't want to waste time and resources. They have got real crimes to tackle.'

By the time the hunting season officially opened on 5 November 2005, there had already been many weeks of hunting since the Act came into force. Some 50 allegations of illegal hunting had been made to the police by the League Against Cruel Sports, and a small number of these were referred to the Crown Prosecution Service. Not one led to a prosecution for the simple reason that there was insufficient evidence of a crime being committed. This is not to say that some of the hunts were not hunting illegally. Some might have been.

Many activities involving hounds and other types of dog remain legal. For example, you can exercise hounds; you can follow an artificial trail with a full pack of hounds; you can flush wild mammals to guns, unless they are protected species and provided you use two hounds or less; and you can use dogs for 'exempt hunting', such as the pursuit of rabbits or rats. It is extremely difficult for the police, or for that matter anybody else, to distinguish between these legal activities and those which have been banned under the Act, and it is even more difficult to prove the intention of the hunters, rather than the dogs.

Anyone who wishes to ridicule the Act, and test it to the limits, will have no trouble doing so. Take, for example, the hunting of hares. It is illegal under the Act to hunt hares with dogs. However, you can hunt hares with as many hounds as you like providing you are pursuing hares which have been shot. This raises the extra-ordinary possibility of people taking pot shots at hares and wounding them lightly enough not to kill them, thus making them legitimate quarry for a proper hunt. As far as I know, nobody has attempted to do this, but hunts have exploited another loophole which allows them to flush wild mammals so they can be hunted by birds of prey. This also raises welfare concerns. By November 2005, some 40 hunts were using harrier hawks, eagle owls, golden eagles and other birds of prey. This practice was deplored by the Hawk Board on the grounds that it prejudices the welfare of the birds. There are also welfare implications for foxes caught by birds of prey, as they are unlikely to die as swiftly as they would when caught by a pack of hounds. However, the real implications of the Act for the welfare of the fox and other traditionally hunted animals are far more serious than this.

We would never have ended up with this unworkable piece of legislation if MPs who were ideologically in favour of the ban had visited the countryside, witnessed hunts at work and talked to farmers and others about alternative methods of controlling foxes and deer. We might have ended up with a very different piece of legislation, one which proscribed certain activities and sanctioned hunting under licence, but we would certainly not have ended up with a law which will make matters worse, not better, for animal welfare. A pitifully small number of anti-hunting or agnostic MPs were broad-minded enough to visit their local hunts or talk to people involved in fox control. Among those who did were Barry Sheerman, Labour MP for Huddersfield, Austin Mitchell, Labour MP for Grimsby and Lembit Öpik, Liberal MP for Montgomeryshire. All three now support or are members of the All Party Parliamentary Middle Way Group. It is important to stress that they are not so much pro-hunting as anti-cruelty.

It is also important to stress that prejudice was not confined to one side. Many pro-hunting MPs and pro-hunting members of the House of Lords buried their heads in the sand and refused to accept that some aspects of hunting were problematic from the point of view of animal welfare, and that this justified some form of reformist legislation. Fortunately, a small number of brave souls stuck their heads above the parapet and made it plain to their colleagues that the status quo – self-regulation by the hunters – was simply unacceptable. Among the more notable was Lord Willoughby de Broke, who originally championed self-regulation, then realised that this wasn't a political option, and became a keen supporter of the Middle Way Group. For this he was much rebuked by certain pro-hunting members of the House of Lords.

Lembit Öpik's conversion away from a hunting ban dates from his meetings with the David Davies Hunt in his mountainous and sheep-rich constituency in mid-Wales. He sat in the house of the huntsman David Jones, within noisy earshot of the kennels, and listened to a countryman describing the business of how the countryside actually works, in terms of its ecology and economy, and the complex relationships between man and nature, predator and prey.

When I arrived at the kennels in mid-July 2005, Jones was skinning two horses and a heifer, fallen stock which he had collected that morning. He washed the sweat from his forehead and the blood from his hands and we talked about the effect the Hunting Act will have on the fox.

This is one of those areas where hunting with dogs is the most efficient form of fox control. This was made absolutely clear in the Burns Report. Every year the David Davies Hunt kills between 160 and 200 foxes. During the hunting season, the hunt goes out once a week on horseback, and once or twice a week on foot. Most of the followers are local farmers. Jones also takes his hounds out on lambing calls. These involve the early-morning pursuit of a particular fox which has recently killed a lamb or lambs. The year after the foot-and-mouth outbreak, Jones answered 57 lambing calls, and got every fox. From an economic point of view, this is a vital service. 'Last year,' he recalled, 'one of our farmers lost 10 lambs in three nights to a fox. That amounted to a loss of around £500.' Without the use of scent hounds, Jones could never have been sure that he had tracked down and killed the guilty fox.

So how did he expect the Hunting Act, which had recently

come into force, to affect the fox population in these mountains? For one thing, replied Jones, if he decided to abide by the law he would only be able to take two hounds out on each lambing call, and then he would have to flush foxes to a gun. This would be inefficient and sometimes impractical, for two reasons. First, it is far more efficient to pursue a fox with 30 or more hounds, rather than just two, for the simple reason that different hounds have different qualities: some have good noses, some are better at catching the fox, others at pursuing. Second, using a firearm to kill a fox is an inherently dangerous activity in hilly terrain full of livestock, as the Burns Report concluded. However, Jones felt that he was unlikely to be as badly affected by the Hunting Act as the 14 gun packs which operate in his hunting country. Gun packs use dogs to drive foxes towards guns. It would be almost impossible for them to act within the law and remain an efficient form of fox control, suggested Jones. A leaked memo, dated 22 July 2005, from the League Against Cruel Sports' chief executive, Douglas Batchelor, pointed out that 'gun packs have realised that pairs of dogs are utterly useless at flushing to guns from forestry plantations or in the fells.' So it seems that even the anti-hunting lobby have concluded this form of 'exempt hunting' is of doubtful value for pest control.

'What this means is that farmers will use whatever methods they can to kill foxes,' said Jones. 'Some of the methods they use will be legal, like shooting and snaring, but these often cause much greater suffering than hunting.' To prove his point, he showed me some photographs of snared and shot foxes. One of the foxes had a snare round its belly and had been half eviscerated, having dragged the wooden plank to which the snare was attached for days before it was eventually found and dispatched. Another, a vixen, had been shot through the head. According to a veterinary report commissioned by Jones, 'the tongue is completely severed ... the right eye cannot be located ... there is a compound fracture of the orbital rim.' The vixen survived like this for several days before it was dispatched by a hunt.

Jones anticipated that farmers would also resort to the use of poison. Some already had. 'The Hunting Act takes no account of human nature,' he said by way of explanation. Poisons are easily available to farmers, and there is nothing simpler than adding poison to the carcass of a dead lamb or rabbit and leaving it out for a fox to devour. Besides leading to an agonising death for the fox, poisoned bait will also lead to the death of other wildlife. As we talked, Jones pointed to a goshawk that soared across the hillside. 'If there's more poisoning,' he reflected, 'it won't just be goshawks and red kites and buzzards that die, it'll be all the small birds, the goldfinches and songbirds, that peck around carcasses in search of animal fat as well.'

On my way back to London I called in on Patrick Martin, huntsman for the Bicester with Whaddon Chase in Oxfordshire. He reckoned the Hunting Act was already having a negative impact as far as animal welfare was concerned. 'Some of the farmers round here already believe that the Hunting Act will mean that fewer foxes will be killed by hunts when the season begins, so they have been shooting foxes themselves,' explained Martin. The most effective time to cull foxes is during the spring and early summer, as this has the greatest impact on population growth. This is also the time when they cause the greatest problems for farmers. Martin had recently found a wet vixen – a female still nursing young – which had been shot. 'What that means is four or five cubs will have starved to death. And there will be dozens more suffering the same fate. It's bloody cruel. Period.' It is not, however, illegal.

If the MPs who were so eager for a ban had bothered to do their research properly, they would have known that this would happen. The Game Conservancy Trust looked at the impact gamekeepers had on the fox population in certain parts of the country.[11] In 1996, a sample of 60 gamekeepers killed 707 vixens, 179 during the period when foxes breed. Efforts were made to kill the cubs at the earths of 39 of these vixens, but the Trust calculated that over 160 cubs were likely to have died through lack of maternal care. They would have slowly starved to death.

'I have never wounded a fox in my life,' said Martin, whose hunt kills some 220 foxes each year. 'When we hunt, the fox either dies, or it escapes unharmed.' Now, however, the Hunting Act obliged him to pursue foxes with just two dogs and flush them to guns. Some foxes will inevitably be wounded and left to die a lingering death. 'I am now being encouraged to use a form of control that has the potential to cause wounding,' he said. 'This Hunting Act amounts to nothing more than government-sponsored cruelty.'

CHAPTER 2

Corrupting the Evidence

The fact that a great many MPs failed to scrutinise the available evidence does not mean that it was without significance. Those who made the running in the debates, whether in favour of hunting or against, made as much use as they could of expert opinion, especially the written and oral evidence presented at the Burns Inquiry and at the Portcullis House hearings. Of course, there was a great deal of cherry-picking, with the protagonists choosing whichever bits of evidence best suited their case. But the evidence, and its integrity, mattered. If you have any doubts about this, you need look no further than the High Court judgement on a challenge to the Hunting Act brought by the Countryside Alliance and others in the summer of 2005.[1]

The Countryside Alliance and its co-claimants objected to the Act on various grounds. They claimed, among other things, that it was 'disproportionate' and an unnecessary and illegitimate interference with their rights to choose how they conducted their lives. They also argued that the legislation was irrationally enacted and would result in more cruelty, rather than less. In their view, wild mammals like foxes and red deer would now be killed by methods that inflicted greater pain and suffering than hunting with hounds.

There was nothing remotely equivocal about the findings of Lord Justice May and Mr Justice Moses. They maintained that there was sufficient material available to the House of Commons for MPs to conclude that hunting with dogs was cruel. 'There was, in any event,' wrote the judges, 'a reasonable basis on the evidence for a conclusion that, taken as a whole, hunting foxes with dogs causes more suffering than shooting them.' Hence the ban was justified. The case against hunting, according to the judges, was even more persuasive as far as deer, hare and mink were concerned.

It was widely accepted by MPs who favoured a ban on hunting that foxes and other hunted quarry would still be subject to culling after a ban came into force. As Lord Burns told the Portcullis House hearings: 'farmers will control the number of foxes by one means or another whether there is a hunting ban or there is not a hunting ban … What we are talking about is the alternative methods by which they die.' Many of the organisations and some of the scientists who favoured a ban claimed to have evidence which clearly proved that shooting was a humane alternative to hunting with dogs. My contention in this chapter is that some of this evidence was seriously flawed. The judges who rejected the Countryside Alliance's judicial challenge to the Hunting Act, and MPs who voted for the legislation on the basis of this evidence were therefore actively misled.

When presented with conflicting evidence on complex issues, MPs face the difficult task of deciding where the truth lies. Most have little or no scientific training, and their task is made all the harder when presented with evidence of dubious value. Anybody who takes time to read through the massive body of material related to hunting – the High Court judges were presented with 32 lever-arch files – will be struck by the way in which conjecture, when repeated often enough and without appropriate qualification, can develop a veneer of respectability it has not earned. Scientists have a responsibility to present evidence which is objective, clearly described and based on sound research. Yet some of the most crucial areas of discussion in the hunting debate were sullied by the misrepresentation of facts and the abuse of science.

There has been plenty of research on the ecology of the three main hunted species: fox, red deer and hare. If you want to know about their diet, or their sex lives, or the ways in which populations fluctuate, you will find no end of peer-reviewed papers in scientific journals. However, there is a remarkable paucity of information about the impact which hunting and other methods of control have on the welfare of individual animals. 'When it comes to the issue of foxes,' said Lord Burns at the Portcullis House hearings, 'I was particularly struck – considering the emotion that was generated by this whole debate – by how really very little science has been done, either in terms of the welfare effects of hunting or indeed the other methods of control.'

In fact, the only comprehensive research investigating the impact of hunting on live quarry, in terms of animal welfare, has been done on red deer in the West Country, and the results were far from conclusive. In 1996, the National Trust, a major landowner in Exmoor and the Quantocks, commissioned a study by Professor Patrick Bateson FRS on the welfare of hunted deer. Bateson, an ethologist and Provost of King's College Cambridge, and his colleague Dr Elizabeth Bradshaw reported back to the National Trust in 1997.[2] The authors concluded that hunting caused considerable suffering, and the Trust immediately banned the hunting of red deer on its land.

However, Bateson's report immediately came in for heavy criticism. There was some concern about the way in which blood samples had been collected and transported; but more worrying, in the eyes of many veterinarians and exercise physiologists, was the interpretation of the data. Another research project was commissioned and funded by the Countryside Alliance and the Devon and Somerset Staghounds. This was led by Roger Harris, now Professor of Exercise Physiology at University College Chichester, and it became known as the Joint Universities study (R&W Publications, 1999). The JU study investigated the immediate post-hunt blood and muscle pathology of hunted deer, as Bateson and Bradshaw had. The JU study also investigated the animal's locomotory system to gain an insight into how deer respond to being chased, and widened the pathology investigations to include the kidneys. The

JU study also used more refined techniques than Bateson and Bradshaw to investigate muscle pathology.

The JU study found that stag-hunting proceeded with a series of disturbances, which eventually led to a complete loss of muscle carbohydrate and, as Roger Harris explained to the Portcullis House hearings, 'the muscles essentially run out of petrol'.[3] Roger Harris's team estimated that this probably happened when there were twenty minutes of active hunting left. While Bateson and Bradshaw believed that the muscle changes were clear evidence of suffering, Harris's team concluded that the changes which took place were similar to those which occurred in horses and long-distance runners after intensive and prolonged exercise: the deer would experience un-pleasant feelings which could be defined as suffering, but then so did long-distance runners, who happily come back for more of the same. The implications of this were stark: the National Trust had introduced a hunting ban on the back of dubious scientific evidence.

The subsequent debate between the different groups of scientists, and others who had an interest in supporting one side and dismissing or challenging the findings of the other, was lengthy and acrimoni-ous, but Bateson and Roger Harris agreed to collaborate on a joint review of their findings for the Burns Inquiry.[4] They agreed that by the end of the hunt there was clear evidence of very low levels of carbohydrate in the deer's muscles, and this largely explained why the deer stopped running. 'Many of the physiological characteristics of deer at the end of the hunt resemble those for a human or horse involved in a prolonged bout of continuous or intermittent intense exercise,' they concluded. This was a dramatic revision of the original claims made by Bateson and Bradshaw. Indeed, the conclusions relating to some significant parameters measured by Bateson and Bradshaw for their 1997 study were comprehensively modified in the joint study undertaken for the Burns Inquiry in 2000.[5]

It is important to distinguish between fact and opinion. For example, the 2000 paper included the following observation. 'Taken together with the physiological effects of hunting, it is clear that hunting with hounds would not be tolerated in other areas of animal husbandry if considerations such as sporting interests and population management were ignored.' Bateson included this sentence in a letter to Charles Nunneley, the chairman of the National Trust, in which he maintained that the 2000 joint study with Roger Harris reaffirmed the key conclusions of his 1997 report with Elizabeth Bradshaw. But as Roger Harris pointed out in a letter to Nunneley, they didn't.[6] Harris also pointed out that this was an opinion and not a scientific conclusion. He added: 'Knowing the injuries and distress that can result from shooting, the sentiment of the statement could apply equally well to the stalking of deer.'

As the veterinary experts Dr Lewis Thomas and Professor W.R. 'Twink' Allen stated in their written evidence to the High Court of Justice in April 2005, the claim that hunting with hounds would not be tolerated in other areas of animal husbandry went far beyond anything justified by the findings of the two experimental studies, and suggested an imperfect knowledge of animal husbandry.[7] 'Our experience is that in market places, transportation carriers and slaughterhouses,' wrote the vets, 'stress and disturbance greatly exceeds what might be experienced in the hunting field.'

Lord Burns provided a somewhat equivocal summary of the research findings. He pointed out that although there were still substantial areas of disagreement, there was now better understanding of the physiological changes which took place when deer were hunted. However, he then went on to say: 'Most scientists agree that deer are likely to suffer in the final stages of hunting.' This was not strictly true: Roger Harris and his colleagues suggested that towards the end of a hunt, hunted deer experienced the sort of feelings which would be familiar to anyone who has run fast or for a long time. Lord Burns added that the available evidence 'does not enable us to resolve the disagreement about the point at which, during the hunt, the welfare of the deer becomes seriously compromised.' Nevertheless, his view was that hunting did cause a significant degree of suffering towards the end of the chase.

Let us suppose that to be the case. Does it automatically mean that stag-hunting should be banned? Yes, suggested Alun Michael. Yes, said the coalition of anti-hunting groups. But the suffering of a hunted deer – about which we remain unclear – must be weighed against the suffering which would be caused by alternative methods of control if and when hunting ceases. If shooting were to cause greater suffering, then the argument in favour of a ban would be weaker. When done properly, as Lord Burns pointed out, an accurate shot from a stalker is the quickest and cleanest way to kill deer. However, when all the shots that wound, but fail to kill, are taken into account, the totality of suffering – this was the expression used by Professor John Webster, one of the Portcullis House hearings witnesses – might be greater than the suffering experienced by herds of deer which are subject to hunting.

To establish whether or not this is true, we need evidence. Unfortunately, the evidence is inconclusive. For example, Arthur Lindley of the Campaign for the Protection of Hunted Animals cited at the Portcullis House hearings one study which found rifle or shot wounds in between 0.6 and 1.8 per cent of 1,000 deer carcasses, and another study which suggested that less than two per cent of 5,000 culled deer had not been killed instantly. Roger Harris, on the other hand, pointed out at the hearings that his small data set showed alarmingly high wounding rates. Twelve deer were stalked for the JU study by excellent marksman, and the fate of each is known. None was shot in the head. Four were fully conscious and aware of their surroundings, but were unable to move. These deer had to have their throats slit to render them unconscious. Another deer was found after a 20-minute search, fully conscious but paralysed. It had to be shot again. All of this suggests that even when expert marksmen are responsible for stalking deer, death can be a slow and uncertain business.

Bateson and Bradshaw estimated that 14.6 per cent of deer were not killed outright by the first shot, and they suggested that some 70 per cent of those wounded would experience stress analgesia

– an absence of pain – just as 70 per cent of soldiers are reported to do when shot in battle. However, as Thomas and Allen have pointed out, this will provide little comfort to the 30 per cent of deer which would suffer acute pain and distress when wounded. It also ignores the fact that soldiers are shot with hard-nosed bullets that caused much less tissue damage than the soft-nosed bullets used by stalkers, and banned for use in war under the Geneva Convention.[8]

This story illustrates how difficult it is to conduct research on suffering, particularly on live animals in field conditions. It also highlights the way in which different scientists may interpret much the same data in an entirely different way. But most significantly, it shows what happens when decisions are made on the basis of contentious, or disputed, scientific opinion. The National Trust banned stag-hunting on its land because it considered the evidence presented by Bateson and Bradshaw to be credible and trustworthy. Although Bateson continued to assert that his findings were proof of suffering, he significantly revised his interpretation of the data. Had the National Trust been presented with the 2000 paper by Bateson and Harris, I doubt whether it would have felt there were sufficient grounds on which to ban hunting.

But has this mattered as far as red deer are concerned on Exmoor and the Quantocks? Almost certainly. In 2001, Charles Harding, in his capacity as stalker for the Holnicote Estate, wrote to the National Trust's regional chairman for Wessex.[9] He pointed out that there had been an increase in sick and wounded deer found on the estate since the ban on stag-hunting. 'I feel that if the National Trust let the staghounds draw some of the coverts to find these animals, before they die their dreadful lingering death, it would not only be obviously beneficial to the deer but would go some way to regaining the sorely lost cooperation of the tenants and neighbours due to a hunt ban,' he wrote. The fact that the hunt no longer came on the estate meant that deer were no longer dispersed and now congregated in certain areas, causing severe damage of the vegetation. He concluded his letter: 'All types of animal management involve compromises. There is no doubt that a total ban on stag-hunting has increased the number of sick and injured deer on Holnicote Estate, it has gone on long enough. It is about time for the National Trust to accept these consequences and be prepared, for the sake of the deer, to be brave enough to step forward and allow hounds to draw some coverts.'

Several generations hence, historians will be able to look back at the hunting legislation enacted by the Labour government, and the various processes which led to its passage, with a degree of objectivity. They will probably be struck by the eagerness with which many politicians espoused what Roger Scruton terms 'totalitarian sentimentality'; by the contempt in which many urban MPs held a rural minority – one suspects they would have defended their right to live as they pleased had they come from Papua New Guinea, rather than the Cotswolds or the Welsh Marches, and dressed in hide and feathers, rather than Barbour jackets and cloth caps; by the unworkability and lack of logic of the Hunting Act; and by the remarkably small number of expert witnesses who contributed to the debate and shaped its outcome.

Some of the key witnesses appeared before both the Burns Inquiry and the Portcullis House hearings. By far the most persuasive in favour of a ban was Stephen Harris, Professor of Environmental Sciences at Bristol University. Leaving aside his wide experience – a former chairman of the Mammal Society, Stephen Harris has conducted an enormous amount of work on foxes – it is easy to see why the Campaign for the Protection of Hunted Animals was keen to call on the services of the Bristol scientist. At various times, Stephen Harris had been commissioned by the organisations which favoured a hunting ban to conduct research, and he clearly believes hunting to be cruel and unnecessary. He has attended open weekends organised by the League Against Cruel Sports and he was even pictured in a newspaper standing outside the House of Commons on 28 November 1997, applauding Michael Foster after the MP had introduced his Private Member's Bill to ban hunting in 1997.

Stephen Harris was one of the stars of the Portcullis House hearings, giving evidence on six separate occasions, twice as many as anybody else. On the first day, when the hearings were devoted to a discussion of Alun Michael's principle of utility, Harris followed Lord Burns, who opened the proceedings with an account of the findings of his inquiry. He was back in the afternoon, providing a counter view to Dr Jonathan Reynolds of the Game Conservancy Trust on the need to control wild mammals such as the fox. Both these witnesses appeared again later in the day. The following day, when the hearings considered the principle of least suffering, Stephen Harris was called upon to discuss the methods of control that are most humane. He was a key witness again during the afternoon session. On the final day, when the hearings considered how best to apply the principles of utility and least suffering, he was once again a significant contributor.

Equally at ease discussing methods of controlling mink, the necessity or otherwise of population control for foxes and the kindest ways of culling deer, Stephen Harris proved himself an adept all-rounder. Sympathetic foxes would probably describe him as a Renaissance man. He was also articulate and witty. In short, when reading the evidence, future historians will be impressed by him as a performer. But what about the quality of his evidence?

One of Stephen Harris's great strengths is that he understands the importance of providing information in an accessible and journalistic form. Decision-makers and politicians do not want to consult the pages of obscure journals found only in the libraries of universities and research institutes. They want science to be served up in a way that is intelligible and easy to digest. Successful pressure groups such as Greenpeace and the League Against Cruel Sports have always understood this, even if most scientists haven't.

In 1997, presumably in anticipation of a Labour victory and legislation to ban hunting, Stephen Harris and colleagues wrote *Is the fox a pest?* and *How will a ban on hunting affect the British fox population?*[10] These publications were highly influential and became part of the campaign literature of the anti-hunting movement. They were written in an accessible language, yet they retained an air of authority. Their message was clear: fox-hunting was unnecessary; it was also cruel.

But not everyone was impressed. One of Stephen Harris's more articulate adversaries at the Portcullis House hearings, Jonathan Reynolds of the Game Conservancy Trust, provided a critique of *Is the fox a pest?* for a country sports magazine.[11] Reynolds took exception to the report on a number of grounds. He pointed out that it had been funded by a political lobby group, IFAW, and selectively released to the press, but denied to everyone else for a week, in a way which would achieve maximum publicity and engender the least dissent, shortly before the second reading of Michael Foster's Private Member's Bill. *Is the fox a pest?* is presented as a definitive summary of existing research, but is nothing of the sort. It was neither published in a scientific journal nor peer-reviewed, and much of the evidence was unsatisfactory, according to Reynolds. For example, over half the references cited were for publications which had not been refereed, for unpublished reports and for word-of-mouth communications. 'This may sound objective,' wrote Reynolds, 'but it means that evidence of first class experimental studies is ranked equal with that of poor studies that lack any experimental design at all.' One of the references, frequently quoted by the anti-hunting lobby, referred to work conducted in the late 1980s on fox predation on lambs in Scotland which implied that foxes were an insignificant cause of lamb mortality. This was so seriously flawed that it was never published in a scientific journal. It only saw the light of day because it was published as a pamphlet by the League Against Cruel Sports.

Tellingly, Reynolds found that Stephen Harris and his colleagues had misinterpreted research published by his organisation, the Game Conservancy Trust. He concluded his critique with the warning: 'Arguably the greatest sin in this report is to suggest that science has already supplied the answers to the fox controversy. This is not the case. Science has only begun to address some of the issues adequately, and the human/fox relationships will probably require continual reassessment.'

The Game Conservancy Trust also took issue with *How will a ban on hunting affect the British fox population?* The report, written by Stephen Harris and Phil Baker, claimed that current fox control had no impact on fox numbers, except locally. The Game Conservancy Trust pointed out that its own research contradicted this: in large regions, the size of counties or groups of counties, fox control had a substantial impact on fox numbers. The Game Conservancy Trust also contested the report's claim that fox numbers in Britain were in balance with their food supply. In areas such as west Norfolk and mid-Wales – where the Game Conservancy Trust had been conducting research – fox numbers were suppressed as a result of intense culling over a long period of time. It concluded: 'The contribution of hunting with hounds and terriers to the total regional cull of foxes varies between 11 per cent (West Norfolk) and 73 per cent (mid-Wales). 73 per cent seems rather significant to us, and we cannot dismiss the consequences of a ban on hunting foxes with dogs either for regional fox numbers, or for effective local management of fox predation.'[12]

How will a ban on hunting affect the British fox population? contains the earliest reference I can find in the UK literature to research carried out in the late 1980s in the United States by Dr Terry Kreeger and colleagues. The way this research has been used by anti-hunting scientists and campaigners is highly instructive and worth examining at some length. It provides clear evidence that some scientists and lobbying organisations have misinterpreted research to suit their own ends.

Stephen Harris and Baker first used the US research in the following way, when answering the claim, commonly made by the hunting lobby, that hunted foxes are either killed outright or escape unharmed: 'This argument implies that there is no cruelty in the hunt, but studies in North America have shown that hunting a fox for five minutes in a ten acre enclosure causes as much physiological suffering as catching an animal in a leg-hold trap. Leg-hold traps have been banned in England and Wales for 40 years because they are so cruel.' In other words – and it is impossible to read this statement any other way – the American research proves that chasing foxes with dogs causes as much suffering as a method of trapping banned in the UK in the 1950s.

The two studies on which Stephen Harris and Baker based this statement were entirely separate. The first used radio implants to measure body temperature and heart rates in foxes for various activities, including sleeping, being awake, foraging, feeding, running and being chased. The scientists found that heart rates and body temperature increased with the level of activity. The findings of this research – 'not quite of Nobel Prize-winning calibre!' as Kreeger later commented[13] – were published in 1989 in the *Canadian Journal of Zoology*.[14] The second piece of research looked at the physiological responses of foxes to capture in foothold traps and box traps. The scientists measured temperature and heart rates, as they had in the previous study, but they also conducted post-mortem examinations of internal organs and blood chemistry. This research was published in 1990 in the *Journal of Wildlife Management*.[15]

Anyone who has bothered to read these two papers will realise that it is impossible to confuse them, other than mischievously. However, it seems that Stephen Harris and Baker, when writing *How will a ban on hunting affect the British fox population?* failed to consult either. Instead they relied – and this is the only reference they cite – on an animal rights website.[16] The website had transferred the pathological findings of the 1990 study on trapped foxes to the 1989 study on chased foxes. By accepting at face value statements made on an overtly propagandist website, Stephen Harris and Baker perpetuated the errors made by the website.

They were not the only ones to do so. In its submission to the

Burns Inquiry, the RSPCA quoted Stephen Harris and Baker almost word for word, before adding the conclusively damning statement: 'on post-mortem the foxes showed haemorrhage of heart and lungs and congestion of the adrenal glands and kidneys. Blood analyses showed high levels of enzymes reflecting tissue damage.' The RSPCA submission implied that this was what happened to foxes that were being chased by dogs. If true, it would indeed have been a terrible indictment of hunting. But it wasn't true. The post-mortem findings referred to the trapped foxes of the other study.

Kreeger's studies were also misused by IFAW in its submission to the Burns Inquiry, and in an article in the *Sunday Times* on 14 November 1999. The article stated that 'new research claims for the first time that hunted foxes suffer fatal stress levels even if they escape the hounds,' and that foxes chased by dogs 'suffered from muscle myopathy, a muscle-wasting condition that can be followed by brain damage, paralysis and death.' It also claimed that Kreeger had concluded 'that a hunted fox experiences significant stress and possible heart, lung and liver damage before it dies.'

Kreeger, a wildlife vet with the Wyoming Game and Fish Department, wrote to the *Sunday Times* refuting all these claims. He pointed out that there was no evidence of myopathy in any of the chased foxes, and that claims for brain damage, paralysis and death were purely speculative. 'Although a chased foxes is physiologically stressed,' he wrote, 'there was no evidence of any heart, lung or liver damage that would lead to mortality.'[17] In correspondence with the Middle Way Group, Kreeger later wrote: 'At no time did we infer that trapped or chased foxes would suffer any morbidity or mortality as a result of being trapped or chased. On the contrary, it was our 'feeling' that the stress of being trapped or chased was probably inconsequential regarding the ultimate survival of the fox.'[18] Kreeger had already attempted to put the matter to rest by writing an open letter to the Burns Inquiry, in which he stated that there had been a continuing problem with interpretation of his data. 'I personally have no stake in this issue in the UK, other than trying to insure that the objective truth is disseminated,' he said.[19]

None of this deterred Stephen Harris from using Kreeger's data once again, this time very publicly, at the Portcullis House hearings. He was asked by John Jackson of the Countryside Alliance whether he was aware of Kreeger's objections to the misuse of his data. He said he was, and then he went on to say: 'I have simply quoted to you exactly the data he published and he shows quite clearly that for that very short activity he tested – and he was trying to look at the cruelty involved with the use of leg-hold traps – being chased by a dog caused much higher levels in the parameters of body temperature and heartbeat than being caught in a leg-hold trap for two hours. That is quoting directly from his paper. That is published information and you can have it. I have not drawn any other comparison beyond that … I have been quite honest.'

This all sounds reasonable. But it doesn't tally with the claims Stephen Harris made in his written submission to the Portcullis House hearings. He began the relevant discussion in his paper as follows: 'Limited data available on this issue show that being pursued by a dog for five minutes (roughly half the average hunt time) led to considerably higher heart rates and body temperatures than recorded during any other activity (Kreeger et al., 1989). In fact the parameters they recorded were considerably higher than those recorded in foxes caught in leg-hold traps (Kreeger et al., 1990).' This is a reasonably fair representation of the two studies. However, Harris immediately went on to state the following: 'Since gin (leg-hold) traps were made illegal in England and Wales in 1958 on welfare grounds, we must assume that the level of suffering experienced during the pursuit phase of fox hunting has already been deemed unacceptable and that to continue to allow this level of suffering would be incompatible with welfare standards for foxes that were set 45 years ago.'

Stephen Harris's conclusions once again misrepresent Kreeger's research findings, and his claim to have interpreted the research honestly appears disingenuous, to say the least. Nothing in Kreeger's studies justifies Harris's contention that hunting causes as much suffering, or more, than the use of leg-hold traps. Higher temperatures and heart rates cannot be taken as an index of suffering. Next time you run for the number 73 bus, check your heart and feel your forehead: your heart will be beating faster, and you'll be significantly hotter than you were before you began your pursuit. In fact, if Harris had read the 1989 paper carefully, he would have seen that four foxes which were running of their own free will had body temperatures higher than the median for chased foxes. If Harris's logic were to be applied consistently, then the Government should ban foxes from running after rabbits – for their own sakes, not for the rabbits.

There was plenty of discussion at the Portcullis House hearings, and plenty of disagreement, about the relative merits, in welfare terms, of shooting and hunting with dogs. Professor Stephen Harris believed shooting to be far superior. 'The most widespread method of fox culling is shooting and is the technique that is perceived to be the most effective by practitioners,' he told the hearings. 'It is humane and it is extremely effective. It is widely argued that there are high levels of wounding with shooting. In fact there is absolutely no evidence at all that this is the case.' He cited research which he and his colleagues had conducted on the health and condition of the British fox population. They had examined 824 foxes which came from a variety of locations around Britain and died from a range of causes. Just five foxes – or 0.6 per cent – showed evidence of old gunshot wounds. Unfortunately, Stephen Harris provided no information in either his written or oral submission about the way in which the foxes were examined. For example, had they been subject to whole-body X-rays, or partial X-rays? Had they been X-rayed at all?

A much better insight into the way in which Stephen Harris has studied wounding rates was provided at a fringe meeting of the Labour Party conference in Brighton on 29 September 2003. The meeting, organised by the Campaign for the Protection of Hunted

Animals, strongly refuted the results of a research project, commissioned by the Middle Way Group and described later in this chapter, which suggested that there was the potential for significant levels of wounding associated with the shooting of foxes.

In an ideal world, the study conducted by Stephen Harris and his colleagues from Bristol University – in an IFAW press release it was called Welfare Aspects of Shooting Foxes in Britain – would be available as a peer-reviewed paper in a scientific journal. At the time of going to press, the research has still not been published, despite the fact that over two years have elapsed since the main findings of the research were announced at the Labour Party conference, and despite various intimations that the research was about to be published.[20] Had it been, I would be able to react to the contents of a peer-reviewed paper, rather than to those of IFAW's three-page summary.

The researchers examined 1,763 X-ray plates from 'over 764 foxes' for signs of shot wounds. These foxes had been admitted to wildlife hospitals 'all over England and parts of Wales'. Stephen Harris and his colleagues found that six foxes had shotgun pellets, two had rifle bullets and 12 had airgun pellets. According to the IFAW summary: 'A total of 80,000 foxes are killed by shooting each year. In addition, just under 4,000 are wounded with shotguns every year and 1,330 wounded with rifles. Surprisingly, the biggest problem appears to be children shooting at foxes with airguns, and approximately 8,650 are wounded in this way each year.' The summary goes on to state: 'The prevalence rate (percentage of the total fox population carrying pellets or bullets) for shotgun pellets, rifle bullets and airgun pellets were 0.9 per cent, 0.3 per cent and 2.0 per cent respectively.'

Leaving aside the fact that the X-rays would be partial body X-rays – if a fox has a broken back leg, you X-ray the leg, not its shoulders or head – and therefore wounds to other parts of the body would not be registered; leaving aside the fact that the foxes admitted to wildlife hospitals would be those amenable to capture, and would not include injured or diseased foxes that had gone to ground, or those from remote places seldom visited by the sort of people who take injured and diseased animals to wildlife hospitals; and leaving aside the claim, presented as irrefutable when in fact it is a much-repeated guesstimate, that 80,000 foxes are killed each year by shooting – leaving all these things aside, the study is still profoundly flawed.

In case you are wondering how Stephen Harris and his colleagues came up with definitive figures for the number of foxes shot by various methods, this is how they made the calculations. Take, for example, their contention that 4,000 foxes are wounded with shotguns every year. The calculation begins with six foxes wounded by shotgun pellets out of 'over 764 foxes' (a figure which is a strange mix of vagueness and precision). This constitutes 0.9 per cent or thereabouts of the foxes investigated. Researchers then assumed a total fox population of England and Wales of around 440,000. 0.9 per cent of this gives you 4,000 foxes wounded by shotguns. Similar calculations have been made for foxes wounded by rifles and air guns.

These calculations make absolutely no sense at all. You simply cannot establish national wounding rates by extrapolating from this small, unrepresentative sample of the 20 X-rayed foxes which have been shot. And as far as the wounding rates cited in the IFAW summary are concerned – 9.1 per cent for shotguns and 3.2 per cent for rifles – this is another case of speculation masquerading as science. The wounding rate is the percentage of total shots fired that wound. How on earth would the researchers know how many shots had been fired at their 'over 764 foxes'? How would they know how many foxes had been wounded and subsequently died unfound? How would they know how many had been shot and wounded, but later restored to full health without visiting a wildlife hospital? They wouldn't.

In short, the research findings, as presented in the IFAW summary, are worthless. The cavalier approach to statistics is extraordinary.

Here is another example. The scientist (and IFAW) state in their conclusions, that 'for every fox currently wounded 16 are killed by dogs'. This means that 223,680 foxes are killed by dogs each year, if you use their figure of 13,980 foxes wounded by shotguns, rifles and airguns. This is clearly nonsense again. Incidentally, it seems strange that animal welfare organisations should make nothing of the fact that 13,980 foxes are wounded by people with guns. In their eagerness to get rid of hunting, and play down the less savoury aspects of shooting, they have ignored the welfare implications of 13,980 foxes wandering around with wounds of varying severity.

The Stephen Harris study of X-rayed foxes, as I mentioned above, was designed – in part, at least – to pour cold water on the worrying conclusions of a study commissioned by the Middle Way Group and led by Dr Nick Fox, a hawk breeder, farmer, skilled marksman and wildlife consultant based in Carmarthenshire. This report, which was later to be published in *Animal Welfare*, the journal of the Universities Federation for Animal Welfare (UFAW), suggested that certain shooting regimes which are quite legal could cause high levels of wounding in foxes.[21]

For obvious reasons, non-military scientists are not allowed to conduct experiments which involve shooting live animals. This meant that Fox and his colleagues had to design a study based on shooting targets. 199 shooters in England, Wales and Scotland, ranging from the highly skilled to the unskilled, used a range of guns and ammunition to shoot at moving life-sized targets of foxes from a range of distances in a range of different conditions. A total of 1,085 gun shots and 885 rifle shots were scored as 'killed', 'seriously wounded', 'lightly wounded' or 'missed' by two pathologists who examined the paper targets, on which the internal anatomy of the fox had been traced.

The main findings were these. Rifles tend to kill more efficiently than shotguns and wound less. However, there is no single regime which causes zero wounding. As a shooter's skill increases, his kill rate increases and miss rate declines. However, his wounding rate stays much the same. The key conclusion of this research is that shooting involves significant levels of wounding, although these vary according to the types of weapon used, the ammunition and the skill of the shooters.

In order to produce results which could be compared with other methods of control – such as poisoning, snaring, hunting and so forth – the scientists devised a 'wounding tax'. This measured the number of foxes that would be wounded for each one killed for the various regimes, distances and skill levels. The lowest wounding tax was 0.1. This applied to the use of various high-powered rifle bullets at distances of 100 and 150 yards by skilled shooters using an armrest. This means that for every 10 foxes killed, one would be wounded (although, of course, it might be killed with a second shot almost immediately, or hunted down by dogs). The highest wounding tax was 13, which applied to the use of a 0.410 gun by semi-skilled shooters at a distance of 25 yards without an armrest. This means that for every fox killed, 13 would be wounded. A more representative shooting regime involved skilled shooters using a 12-bore shotgun with AAA ammunition at a distance of 25 yards without an armrest. This is a regime that meets government guidelines. The wounding tax for this was 1.3, which means that for every 10 foxes killed, 13 would be wounded. To put this in context, the wounding tax for hunting with dogs, when the foxes are hunted and caught (or not caught) above ground, is zero.[22]

Stephen Harris's criticisms of the Middle Way Group study have been publicly aired in the letter pages of *Animal Welfare*. He also provided a synopsis of his criticisms in response to queries from MPs, journalists and others, and he produced a referee's report for the editor of *Animal Welfare*, a copy of which I have seen. Stephen Harris considered the Middle Way Group study – and Fox as a scientist[23] – entirely lacking in merit. Asked by the journal to give a brief assessment of the scientific/technical value of the paper, he responded: 'I do not see any.' Asked to comment on the statistical methods used, he replied: 'Absolutely awful!' Asked whether the work had any benefits or implications for animal welfare, he responded: 'There are none.' Stephen Harris even suggested to Peter Luff, co-chair of the Middle Way Group, that if the report had been an undergraduate study, it would have got a lower second class mark.[24]

In his lengthy letter to *Animal Welfare*, written with his colleague Philip Baker, Stephen Harris says that there is no *a priori* evidence to suggest that the majority of regimes included in the Middle Way Group study 'reflect practices actually occurring in Britain, even if they are legally permissible'.[25] Actually, Fox and his colleagues never make this claim, as they pointed out in their response. Nobody knows how many foxes are shot, and by whom, or using what regimes. Fox and his colleagues had simply tested the regimes which their volunteer shooters said they or others used. The claim made by Baker and Stephen Harris that half of the foxes shot in Britain are killed by gamekeepers, who one would assume are highly skilled, and that gamekeepers were under-represented in the shooting study, was also refuted by Fox and his colleagues. In any case, the Middle Way Group study suggested that although skilled shooters have a higher kill rate, they do not wound much less than unskilled shooters.

Baker and Stephen Harris took great exception to the Middle Way Group study's discussion of wounding rates. They pointed out that when shooters use a rifle or a shotgun, the fox will generally be bowled over if wounded, thus providing an opportunity to shoot a stationary or near stationary target a few seconds later. 'Thus most wounding that does occur is a transitory event with little or no welfare implications,' they suggested.[26] Therefore, the key issue is the number of animals that escape wounded – something which the Middle Way Group study's wounding rate doesn't measure. According to the Bristol scientists, the study implied that around 168,000 foxes would be wounded each year.

Fox and his colleagues considered this a gross abuse of their data. They never suggested that there would be 168,000 foxes wounded each year, and they made this clear in their paper. Their wounding rates relate to the probabilities of wounding for the first shot fired, because this is the only statistically sound starting point: 'The probabilities of further shots or interventions (such as dogs) quickly killing a wounded fox are real, and we have discussed them, but could not measure them.' Fox and his colleagues also pointed out that Baker and Harris misunderstood the concept of a wounding tax, which relates not to the number of shots fired, but the number of foxes wounded for each one killed. Baker and Stephen Harris, in their critique, averaged the wounding taxes across all of the Middle Way Group study shooting regimes – but these regimes were never supposed to represent the spectrum of regimes used on foxes in the UK, so averages are meaningless. Baker and Stephen Harris also assumed that the probabilities for the second shots fired would be the same as for the first shots. This, as Fox has pointed out, is a statistical blunder: the probabilities would be different for a variety of reasons. Foxes which have already been shot at would present themselves differently, would probably be moving faster, and would probably be further away or out of sight than when the first shot was fired.

At the time of the IFAW fringe meeting, in September 2003, the Middle Way Group study existed as a lengthy report which had yet to be the peer reviewed. It was submitted in a shorter form for publication in *Animal Welfare* in April 2004. It was then sent out for peer review. One of the peer reviewers was Stephen Harris, whose highly critical report was effectively rejected by the editorial board. Subject to certain agreed revisions, the other reviewers recommended publication, and the paper was published in May 2005. The paper would not have passed the peer review process unless it was considered conceptually and methodologically sound.

This is not to say that it is a perfect piece of work. It isn't. Shooting at targets, rather than live foxes, is not ideal – but there is no acceptable alternative when conducting experiments on shooting and wounding. Some of the regimes used by the shooters will have been over-represented, and others under-represented. As the shooters knew when and where the targets would appear, the experiment might have actually underestimated the levels of wounding that could occur in real-life situations. We have no idea whether the mix of skilled, semi-skilled and unskilled shooters reflects what really happens in real life. However, we do know that life in the countryside is a messy and often ill-disciplined business.

People who view foxes as vermin – as many do – are primarily concerned with putting them out of business, and will take shots using the wrong weapons at too great a distance in the wrong conditions to be sure of killing outright, or at all. Organised game-bird shoots often instruct participants to shoot any foxes they come across. One major-general of my acquaintance recently told me that he had brought down a fox which had already been shot at and hit by several other guns on a pheasant shoot. As Stephen Harris wrote in one of his submissions for the Portcullis House hearings, foxes 'are often peppered when people are out shooting birds when they are loaded with small shot'. This seems to contradict his more loudly trumpeted contention that wounding is rare, and indeed there is enough evidence to show that the wounding of foxes is not a rare phenomenon, as the unpublished Stephen Harris/IFAW study suggests.

A Danish study found that 25 per cent of 143 rural foxes examined (compared to four per cent of 48 urban foxes examined) carried shotgun pellets.[27] There is no reason to suppose that the Danes are less competent shots than we are. An analysis of 574 shots taken by Scottish gun packs found that almost a third were second shots – which meant they had either missed first time, or were intended as 'cripple stoppers'.[28] And the experience of Scottish hunts – traditional hunting was banned in 2002 in Scotland, but hounds can still pursue foxes providing the latter are killed by shooting, not by the hounds – shows that even skilled marksmen can have trouble finding their target. On a visit to witness Scottish hunting in December 2002, Jim Barrington and Miles Cooper (both formerly of the League Against Cruel Sports) were provided with the following data by the joint-master and huntsman of the Berwickshire Hunt, Jeremy Whaley. Since the beginning of the season, the Berwickshire Hunt had hunted and shot at 22 foxes. Eight were killed outright, nine were missed and escaped, three were wounded and subsequently killed by the hounds, and two were wounded but were never found. Had hunting with hounds been conducted in the traditional manner, there would have been no wounded foxes.

Stephen Harris says that during his studies he has seen several hundred foxes shot at night with a rifle and has yet to see a wounded animal escape. The use of a high-powered rifle at night – a practice known as lamping – is undoubtedly the most effective way to kill foxes under the right conditions, as Lord Burns pointed out. However, Lord Burns went on to state that in certain situations lamping is neither safe nor practical. In places such as these – for example, in the Welsh hills – the alternatives are hunting with dogs, or systems of shooting which are unsatisfactory. 'We received a good deal of evidence arguing that it was not easy to shoot foxes and that a fair number were wounded. We suspect that this is correct,' wrote Burns.

You could argue about the precise figures for wounding rates and wounding taxes provided by the Middle Way Group study, but it is impossible to avoid the conclusion that shooting may cause high levels of wounding. In fact, even Stephen Harris comes close to admitting this in one of his intemperate letters to Peter Luff.[29] 'At best,' he wrote, 'even if the study was scientifically sound, the only conclusion that could be drawn is that there *may* be substantial levels of wounding in foxes and that we now need to look at the situation in the field.' Well, according to the other peer reviewers, the study was scientifically sound.

Had this been nothing more than an interesting scientific spat between two groups of scientists – Stephen Harris and his colleagues at Bristol University on the one hand, and Nick Fox and the co-authors of the Middle Way Group study on the other – I would have afforded it much less space. After all, the hunting debate has thrown up plenty of other examples of the misuse of facts and figures.[30] But this issue of wounding goes to the very heart of the matter, because many MPs voted for a ban on hunting in the firm belief that shooting is a more humane method of control than it is, and that hunting causes more suffering than it does. They believed this because they were presented with evidence that this is the case. Much of this evidence, as I have explained, is deeply flawed. Stephen Harris, in his referee's report on the Middle Way Group's study for *Animal Welfare*, wrote: 'there is no evidence that there is even an animal welfare issue here. The issues are manufactured and I am afraid it is a political issue, not an animal welfare issue.'[31] If anybody was playing politics, it was Stephen Harris and his supporters and sometime paymasters in the animal welfare movement. They launched their tendentious findings at a party political conference; they used them in public forums; they undoubtedly influenced the political process. This is a clear example of the corruption of science for political purposes.

CHAPTER 3

Lobbyists or Liars?

The way anti-hunting organisations used the Burns Report gives a good insight into their skill at manipulating information to their own advantage. Initially, they railed against Jack Straw, the Home Secretary, for setting up the Burns Inquiry and appointing to the committee individuals whom they believed to be sympathetic to field sports. But once the Burns Report was published, they used it brilliantly. To give just one example, the Campaign for the Protection of Hunted Animals' trenchant critique of hunting, *Utility and Cruelty – reasons to ban hunting with dogs*, contains 40 references, 27 of which are to the Burns Report.[1] By leaning so heavily on the report, the Campaign gave the impression that its own case against hunting had received a stamp of approval from an authoritative source. So selective was *Utility and Cruelty* in its use of the Burns Report that the casual reader could be forgiven for thinking that Burns and his colleagues had declared hunting to be an unspeakably cruel pastime. They hadn't, of course. 'Naturally, people ask whether we were implying that hunting is cruel,' said Lord Burns during a debate in Westminster, 'the short answer to that question is no. There was not sufficient verifiable evidence or data safely to reach views about cruelty.'[2]

Most people – many MPs included – never read the Burns Report or listened to the hunting debates. Instead, their views were shaped by sound-bites on the radio, short clips on television, and features and news items in the newspapers. Influencing the media, and getting widespread coverage, was what really mattered, both to organisations campaigning for a ban and those which wished to resist it, and the propaganda war was every bit as important as the debates in the Houses of Parliament and Portcullis House. It was a war which the anti-hunting lobby won hands down.

To convince politicians and the public that hunting should be banned, anti-hunting organisations had to establish a sufficient body of evidence to show that hunting was cruel and unnecessary. They claimed they succeeded. After the Hunting Act was passed, IFAW announced: 'The case for a ban was based on rigorous scientific research that dispelled the myths put forward by the hunting lobby. Scientists and vets proved conclusively that, where control is necessary, there are more humane and efficient methods of dealing with a problem animal.' This bold claim simply doesn't bear examination. The truth is that anti-hunting organisations had no qualms about using the flimsiest and least credible evidence – Stephen Harris's study of X-rayed foxes is an obvious example – to further their cause. They were perfectly willing to corrupt the findings of reputable scientists such as Dr Terry Kreeger in their quest to establish a case against hunting, and selectively to plunder the Burns Report and the Portcullis House hearings in support of their case.

That the League Against Cruel Sports should behave in such a way should come as no surprise. The League has long been passionately opposed to animals being killed for sport. In so far as it has a world view, it is black and white. There are no shades of grey; there is no room for nuance or debate. People who hunt are portrayed as a barbaric and bloodthirsty minority who slay innocent animals, and those who defend them are typecast as myth-makers and liars. The attitude is very much one of you're-either-with-us-or-against-us, as I discovered when I asked for an interview with the League's chief executive when writing *Fox-hunting: Beyond the Propaganda*. I was bluntly told by the press officer: 'That won't be possible. You are writing for a pro-blood sports organisation and there would be nothing to be gained by co-operating with you. You are known as a pro-blood sports journalist.' Strange: I thought I was a impartial observer, albeit with libertarian leanings. As for Wildlife Network, it had been set up by Jim Barrington and several other former League members. The claim that their new organisation was pro-blood sports was ludicrous. But then apostasy is as much of a crime as hunting to the League: Barrington and two other chief executives had quit after deciding that a ban on hunting would make life worse for some hunted species, not better.

Denigration is a key weapon in the League's armoury, and this is well illustrated by the way in which the League has attempted to link hunting with violence. In a letter to the *Daily Telegraph*, the League's chief executive, Douglas Batchelor, had the following to say: 'The FBI, the American Psychiatric Association and others use evidence of cruelty to animals as indicators of personality disorders that can lead to crimes of violence. In other words, maladjusted people using acts of dominance over animals can, and sometimes do, move on to crimes of violence to fellow citizens.'[3]Presumably, this means that huntsmen, whippers-in and those who follow hunts are more likely to slap their spouses, punch their neighbours and make a violent nuisance of themselves than the rest of us. The League has yet to provide hard evidence for this. Indeed, it seems extraordinary that the League should try to clamber on to the moral high ground. As Jim Barrington wrote, in a letter in response to Batchelor: 'When I, as the executive director of the League in the 1990s, questioned a simple ban on hunting with dogs and advocated a better way forward for animal welfare, I was subjected to a stream of abuse and threats of physical violence.'[4]

Batchelor has also sought to link hunting and child abuse.[5] 'I am sure you will agree that people hunt and shoot mostly because they enjoy it,' he wrote to one defender of hunting. 'Our case is quite simply that they should not enjoy it. In much the same way as while paedophiles may feel that they enjoy abusing children and are therefore justified, a civilised society condemns their pleasures and regards them as socially unacceptable in what is now a more civilised society. No amount of argument that it is 'well done' addresses the point that it should not be done at all!' A similar attempt to couple hunting with child abuse and rape was made at the Portcullis House hearings by Reverend Professor Andrew Linzey, whom the League and its allies seem to have adopted as their in-house philosopher.

No-one should be surprised that the League Against Cruel Sports has played fast and loose with the truth, as it has, for example, with its claims that there is evidence of cruelty in the chase of the fox, when in fact there is no evidence either one way or the other. Nor should we be surprised when it adopts a tone of moral outrage, or scatters insults towards its enemies with all the spluttering gusto of a playground bully. To conclude a letter to Alun Michael, the Minister for Rural Affairs, with the exhortation, 'No compromise, no time-wasting, please do what Mr Blair promised two years ago and – just do it – NOW!' may strike you as being on the brash side, but at least the League is always true to type.[6] We know what we are getting, and we know that we should treat its pronouncements with a degree of caution, just as we should those of any campaigning pressure group, including the Countryside Alliance.

But the RSPCA is different. Ask the next person you pass in the street what they think of the organisation, and they will probably give you a glowing, if hazy, tribute – unless, that is, they are sympathetic to field sports and have closely followed the actions and pronouncements of the RSPCA over the last decade or so. The RSPCA has been around for so long, and done so much good, that it has helped to define what we are as a race. If foreigners look upon us as being eccentrically fond of animals, this owes much to the work of the RSPCA. At a parochial level, it acts as a sort of Salvation Army for down-and-out dogs and cats. On the larger canvas, it has helped to pilot some of the key reforms in animal welfare through Parliament. Were it not for the RSPCA, there might still be a live meat export trade in horses across the Irish Sea, much laxer laws governing vivisection, and less scrutiny of animal welfare in livestock markets. Parliament has listened attentively to the advice of the RSPCA because it has made good use of science in championing its cause. And that is how it should be.

However, in recent years, the RSPCA has adopted a hard-line animal rights – rather than animal welfare – approach to field sports, and particularly hunting, and gushy sentimentality and emotion have triumphed over sound judgment and a willingness to make honest use of science. Being a charity, this matters for legal reasons. According to the Chief Charity Commissioner: 'it is open to the RSPCA to argue that hunting involves unnecessary suffering on the basis that, where it is necessary to control numbers, other more humane methods exist.' However, this must be based on 'reasoned argument and evidence, not on the personal viewpoint and emotions of members.'[7]

The evidence presented by the RSPCA in the High Court of Justice in 2005, in defence of the Hunting Act, provides an insight into the slippery way in which the organisation has used, or pretended to use, science to make its case against hunting.[8] After informing the judges that the RSPCA was in a unique position to contribute to the proceedings from the perspective of animal welfare, John Rolls, its director of animal welfare promotion, made the following pronouncements: that the RSPCA did not believe hunting was ever an effective form of control or culling; that the RSPCA did not believe there was any need for foxes to be controlled 'on a national basis'; that the RSPCA did not consider the fox to be 'a general pest'.

Let's take these claims one by one. First, research by the Game Conservancy Trust has shown that in some areas – for example, in the Welsh hills – hunting with dogs is the most effective method of controlling foxes.[9] This was accepted by Lord Burns. The second statement, suggesting that foxes do not need to be controlled, raises two interesting points. If that is the case, why has the RSPCA not argued in favour of the total protection of the fox? And has the RSPCA considered what would happen to foxes if they were not controlled – in other words, if the 100,000 or more animals which are annually shot, hunted and snared were left to die of other causes? It is claimed by those who believe control to be unnecessary that the fox population would 'self-regulate'. That is quite true. However, the behavioural factors which come into play with self-regulation include harassment of subordinates by dominant females, infanticide and cannibalism of subordinate vixens' cubs.[10] The RSPCA's contention that the fox is not a 'general pest' is meaningless. The fact is that in some areas the fox is a pest; in others it isn't – it is impossible to make generalisations about the fox's status as a pest.

In the High Court of Justice, Rolls raised the issue of scientific evidence on a number of occasions. He began by informing the judges: 'Whilst scientific evidence can play an important role in legislating to protect animals, it is not always determinative. The legislature has considered prevailing social, ethical and moral attitudes and, in the Society's view, has been entitled and obliged to do so.' Fair enough: one accepts that there should be a moral dimension to the debate. Later, Rolls claimed: 'The Society believes that it is plain from the evidence and an examination of the hunting process that the quarry is caused to suffer.' Just in case you were in any doubt about this, here is Jackie Ballard, the RSPCA's director-general, in correspondence with Lord Donoughue: 'The RSPCA's policy on hunting, which has been developed over many years on the basis of a large body of scientific and technical advice, is clear...'.[11]

But where, exactly, is the scientific evidence that chasing foxes, or other wild mammals, causes suffering? As we have seen, the only research has been conducted on red deer in the West Country, and it seems that their pathological response to hunting is similar to that of humans after intense and prolonged exercise. Deer may suffer during the final part of the chase – but we do not know for sure. As for the fox, there has been no research whatsoever, with the exception of Kreeger's, on the effects of the chase, or indeed the kill. And Kreeger's research was on foxes in an enclosure, being chased in conditions which bore no resemblance to an open hunting field.

On the subject of shooting and wounding, Rolls made the RSPCA's view clear in the High Court: 'There is no real evidence that shooting wounds large numbers of foxes – and what evidence there is suggests the opposite.' I am not going to rehearse the arguments again, other than to say that the RSPCA, like the League Against Cruel Sports and IFAW dismissed the peer-reviewed research by Nick Fox and his colleagues, and insisted that the work undertaken by Professor Stephen Harris, based on an examination of X-rayed foxes from wildlife hospitals, conclusively proved that shooting caused very low levels of wounding.

In December 2003, the three co-chairs of the Middle Way Group, Peter Luff, Lembit Öpik and Baroness Golding, wrote to the RSPCA, IFAW and the League Against Cruel Sports, acknowledging that the issue of wounding remained controversial and that the two existing studies appeared to contradict one another.[12] 'In the light of these two conflicting reports,' they wrote, 'the suggestion was made on the 28th October that a joint study was undertaken, with methodology accepted by both the Middle Way Group and organisations opposed to hunting. Professor [Stephen] Harris agreed to hold discussions on such a proposal and the IFAW representative also agreed that this was a very important area to clarify.' The Middle Way Group suggested that another meeting should be held to work out a way to proceed with a new study.

The response from the anti-hunting organisations was blunt.[13] They turned down the offer of a joint study and informed the Middle Way Group that they were satisfied with the work currently being carried out by Stephen Harris. Before signing off, they claimed: 'the IFAW-funded study on wounding rates is currently undergoing peer review and awaiting publication.' That was over two years ago now. The research has yet to be published, and a succession of requests by Lembit Öpik and his colleagues has failed to elicit from the RSPCA scientific references to back up its frequent public claims that hunting causes terror, exhaustion and pain.[14]

One suspects the real reason why the RSPCA and its anti-hunting allies refused to develop a joint project into wounding and shooting is because they feared that the results would undermine their case for a ban. 'I am disappointed, but not surprised, by the RSPCA's inability to respond logically, with facts, to the questions I have asked,' says Lembit Öpik. 'I am not surprised, because the answers to my questions would require them to change their position. The RSPCA was so entrenched in its support for a ban that it was willing to achieve it at the cost of increasing animal suffering in the countryside.'

The correspondence between Lembit Öpik and Jackie Ballard failed to provide the MP with the information he requested, but it did inspire the RSPCA's director-general to make the following statement: 'As you will be aware it is impossible to prove, absolutely, suffering in another living thing, even in another human. There is not absolute proof that wounded foxes suffer, yet it is a basic assumption of the Middle Way Group's position that they do.'

Does this mean that a farmer who was previously reluctant to shoot at a distant fox for fear of wounding it need no longer have any such qualms? If he accepts the Ballard thesis, he can certainly fire away with a somewhat clearer conscience than before. And what about those individuals who enjoy setting terriers on foxes? Such people do exist, after all, and Ballard's strange pronouncement will provide them with some comfort when they meet their maker and are asked to justify their follies and crimes.

Lembit Öpik was bemused. 'So what exactly is the RSPCA for if its director-general thinks that wounding does not necessarily cause suffering?' The Veterinary Association for Wildlife Management was just as perplexed. 'The astonishing statement by the director-general of the RSPCA that there is no absolute proof that wounded foxes suffer hardly seems worthy of comment,' they wrote. 'Most people would assume that an injured fox with a gangrenous wound or a broken leg as a result of shooting was suffering, and would not seek proof of that.'[15]

Strictly speaking, of course, there is no absolute proof that animals ever suffer from any experience at all – lacking the power of speech, they are unable to describe their feelings – but the evidence we have tells us that they do suffer, though not in the same way as humans. There is every reason to believe that animals which have been seriously wounded feel pain, just as we do. However, the part of the brain which is responsible for reflection in humans, the prefrontal cortex, is virtually absent in animals. The species we hunt do not have an awareness of self or the power to reflect, as we have, and it is unlikely they experience what we understand as fear, or mental suffering, when hunted. This helps to explain why foxes which have escaped from hounds – as eight out of 10 do – often revert to their normal types of behaviour soon afterwards. The animal welfare expert Professor John Webster suggests that those foxes that survive the hunt 'learn by experience to cope with the stress of the hunt, expect to escape, and thus may not experience the distress arising from the perception that they are failing to cope until the very last seconds.'[16]

A couple of years ago, the Middle Way Group tried to calculate how much money had been spent on anti-hunting campaigns by the RSPCA, IFAW and the League Against Cruel Sports. It came up with a total of just under £30 million as the expenditure between 1997 and 2002. The RSPCA, it calculated, was responsible for around £15 million. The Middle Way Group admitted that these were estimates, based on annual accounts, and said it was willing to adjust the totals accordingly, if supplied with the correct figures. None of the organisations responded, although these figures have since been used in the national press. Clearly, vast sums of money were spent on the campaign to ban hunting, particularly by the RSPCA.

In the view of Peter Luff, the RSPCA's high-profile anti-hunting campaign has seduced many members of the public into thinking that hunting is the worst form of animal cruelty imaginable. 'Although these people are in a minority, as opinion polls show most people did not want hunting banned,' he wrote to Jackie Ballard in August 2005, 'all this has had the knock-on effect of inverting the public's moral scales, so that it is now possible for someone to think hunting is cruel, but quite cheerfully keep their dog locked away in a tower block or buy battery chickens at £2.50 from Tescos.'[17] He wondered whether this explained why the incidence of animal abuse had recently risen, according to the RSPCA's own figures.

What the RSPCA cannot deny is that it has made an enormous and expensive fuss about hunting, an activity which kills relatively few animals, and remained silent on other issues of major importance for animal welfare. Take the most obvious example: the damage and suffering to wildlife caused by domestic cats. By the mid-1990s, there were approximately 9 million cats in Great Britain. According to a review by Nick Fox and Helen MacDonald, British cats kill at least 88 million wild birds and around 164 million small mammals every year.[18] This exceeds the number of wild animals killed by dogs by a factor of over 12,000. What is worse, cats often subject their prey to a gruesomely slow death. In fact, this is the reason why they have been selected as model animals for studies of aggressive predatory behaviour. Overall, cats are responsible for approximately four-fifths of all the kills involving wild animals and birds in Britain. Yet on this issue – and it represents a major conservation problem and a welfare issue which dwarfs hunting – the RSPCA has remained utterly silent.

In fact, for an organisation which makes much of its ethical principles, the RSPCA is remarkably inconsistent. It disapproves of sport angling, which in its view causes pain and suffering, though it has yet to call for its abolition, but it has nothing to say about commercial fishing, where the totality of suffering is presumably much greater. The RSPCA is strongly opposed to hunting with dogs, but it tolerates falconry, which involves setting birds, rather than dogs or ferrets, on other birds or mammals. In its 1997 policy statement it condemned mutilations such as the tail-docking of dogs, but condoned the neutering of pets, which involves the mutilation of sexual organs.[19]

These inconsistencies probably reflect what Jonathan Reynolds, in a critique of an RSPCA policy document, described as a 'confused ethical base'.[20] But one must also assume that there is a strong streak of pragmatism which prevents the RSPCA from highlighting and tackling the damage and cruelty caused by cats. The organisation depends heavily for its funds on the legacies of cat lovers; it simply wouldn't do to offend them. As to its inconsistent position on angling, we can only assume that it has chosen not to attack the sport (yet) because it is enjoyed by some 4 million people in the UK and it has plenty of support in Parliament, not least among prominent anti-hunting MPs, Michael Foster being one.

Incidentally, I was intrigued to see that Jackie Ballard, when interviewed for the *Daily Telegraph* soon after she became chief executive of the RSPCA, said: 'Fishing for food is probably acceptable, but it is cruel to stick a hook in a fish's jaw.'[21] Yet Ms Ballard told the same journalist, Alice Thomson, that she lived on a diet of fruit, vegetables and dolphin-friendly tuna. She has obviously never been on a dolphin-friendly tuna fishing vessel in the Indian Ocean. I have. The fish are caught with a hook, hoiked from the water at great speed and propelled through the air to crash into a wooden holding tank, where they thrash around, often for 20 minutes or more before they die, in a glutinous pool of blood with the rest of the catch. I would rather be a tench or perch periodically pulled out of an English gravel pit, and then returned to go about my fishy business, than one of the tuna which grace Ms Ballard's dining-table.

The RSPCA's opposition to hunting is relatively recent, when seen in terms of its long existence. In its evidence to the Scott Henderson Inquiry, which reported in 1951, the RSPCA's position was that hunting was a more humane method of controlling foxes than shooting. Its views have changed, not because it has had access to scientific evidence that proves shooting to be a more humane method of controlling foxes than hunting, but because the nature of the organisation has changed. Ms Ballard, speaking on Radio 4, described the RSPCA as 'the foremost animal welfare organisation in the country'.[22] This was once true. Now, it is a partial truth. Although the RSPCA still acts as an animal welfare organisation in practical terms – for example, by rescuing maltreated and abandoned animals – it has espoused the philosophy of the animal rights movement. Here, for example, is one paragraph from its Declaration of Animal Rights: 'We believe in the evolutionary and moral kinship of all animals and declare our belief that all sentient creatures have rights to life, liberty and natural enjoyments. We therefore call for the protection of the rights.'[23] If the RSPCA is to remain true to this absolutist declaration, then sooner or later it will campaign for the abolition of shooting and sports fishing, as well as commercial fishing. And it will presumably oppose the killing of rats, mice, cockroaches, blowfly, liver flukes and all the other creatures currently subject to some form of control.

Nobody encapsulates the virtues of the RSPCA as it used to be, before it adopted an animal rights agenda, better than John Hobhouse. Hobhouse is now in his nineties, and he lives in a small village not far from Bath, beside the churchyard where his wife is buried. On her grave is the simple inscription: 'Mary Hobhouse, 1908 – 1991, She was the animals' friend to the end.' It was under his wife's influence, soon after marriage, that Hobhouse became passionately concerned about animal welfare. He was a member of the national council of the RSPCA for 20 years, and national chairman for seven. In his authoritative history of the RSPCA, Anthony Brown wrote: 'For the last few years, the man responsible for guiding the council's policy has been John Hobhouse from an old and much respected liberal family, including two Cabinet ministers. Hobhouse is likely to go down in the Society's history as the first great reforming chairman, who set up detailed specialist committees on factory farming, export of live animals, vivisection, homeless animals ... and introduced top-class scientists whose advice was welcomed by Government ministers.'[24]

Hobhouse was also responsible for establishing a network of cat and dog homes throughout all major towns in the UK. The one with which he is still closely involved, in Bath, temporarily houses and finds home for some 3,000 abandoned or neglected dogs and cats each year. When he first began work with the RSPCA, some 50 years ago, stray dogs were taken to the local vet and put down after seven days if unclaimed. He put an end to the policy of destruction. It would be hard to find anybody who has done more for animal welfare in this country.

I went to see Hobhouse in July 2005 because he had made it known that he was appalled by the RSPCA's attitude towards hunting. 'I'm only pro-hunting in the sense that I think it's less cruel than other methods of control,' he explained. 'Every countryman knows that shooting foxes is often a case of wounding or missing, and the ultimate result is animals slinking away to die from gangrene and their injuries.' The RSPCA, he continued, had given the impression that the 20,000 hounds belonging to registered hunts could be taken in by RSPCA kennels and then re-housed. In theory, they could, but he knew from his own experience that turning a hunting hound into a domestic pet was an arduous and difficult business. 'You're taking an animal that is used to living as part of a pack and eating raw meat,' he explained. 'If you have a dog like that it can take three months or more to get it in into a condition to go into a private home. During that time it's taking up the space that could have been used by half-a-dozen stray dogs.' So the welfare of these six suffers.

In a letter to *The Times*, Hobhouse wrote: 'For an Act of Parliament purporting to relieve animal suffering to do exactly the opposite is very sad. That the RSPCA, which does immensely important work on so many animal welfare fronts, has been party to this fiasco is a tragedy.'[25] It is too early to say quite how much of a tragedy, in terms of animal welfare, the Hunting Act will eventually be. What we do already know is that the manner in which foxes are being killed in areas where hunts have traditionally operated has already changed. By 13 December 2005, 132 hunstmen had responded to a survey which analysed the state of the fox population and methods of culling in use during the autumn.[26] Sixty-nine per cent believed that there had been an increase in the culling of foxes using methods other than hunting with hounds. Seventy-seven per cent cited lamping at night; 36 per cent, other methods of shooting; 16 per cent, snaring; and 5 per cent, other methods. The hunts themselves killed fewer foxes than during the same period the previous year, but the method of culling had changed. Now four out of five foxes killed under Hunting Act exemptions were dug out using terriers, ostensibly to protect game birds; the rest were flushed to guns using two hounds. We do not know how many foxes were killed 'accidentally' by the hounds.

When a fox is hunted with hounds it is either killed, and the kill above ground is almost always swift, or it escapes. The same does not apply to snaring. Shooting can kill swiftly, but shooting wounds as well. Indeed, one of the most remarkable admissions about this came from the British Association for Shooting and Conservation (BASC). In a critique of the shooting and wounding research conducted by Nick Fox and his colleagues, BASC's Jeffrey Olsted suggested that a wounding rate 'of, say, less than 10 per cent' could be accepted as the standard for shooting performance.[27] Let's say 100,000 foxes are shot each year. That means that it would be acceptable – in BASC's view – for 10,000 foxes to be wounded each year. This is (or was) approximately the number of foxes killed above ground each year – killed, mind you, not wounded – by organised hunts before the Hunting Act came into force.

CHAPTER 4

Searching for Solutions

The Hunting Act fails to do what it is supposed to do. Instead of improving animal welfare in the countryside, it is almost certainly causing greater suffering among certain traditionally hunted species, most notably the fox. It is also illogical. For example, it prohibits the hunting of hares with dogs, but allows the hunting of rabbits; it allows the use of terriers to dig out foxes which are a threat to game birds, but bans the use of terriers to dig out foxes which are killing ground-nesting birds such as curlews and terns, or foxes which have been injured, for example by shooting. It has been guided by the belief that killing to control pests is acceptable, but killing for sport is not, yet some of the worst abuses of animals are done in the name of pest control. And it is almost impossible to enforce: witness the lack of prosecutions, despite the efforts of the League Against Cruel Sports and others to draw the attention of the police to malpractice. But the Act was never going to improve animal welfare in the countryside, for the simple reason that its focus is so narrow.

The Hunting Act is primarily concerned with the fate of individual animals, and particularly the manner of their death. It ignores the welfare of individual animals over their lifetime, and it fails to consider the welfare of communities and populations of animals. At the Portcullis House hearings, John Webster, professor of animal husbandry at the University of Bristol, suggested that it was morally inadequate simply to consider welfare in terms of the individual close to the time of its death, as the Hunting Act now does.[1] He suggested we should not only seek to minimise acute suffering immediately prior to death, and minimise extended suffering, for example during a long hunt, but we should also seek to minimise chronic suffering, for example from hunger and disease. This view failed to impress Alun Michael. A pity: had Parliament adopted Webster's holistic vision of animal welfare we might have ended up with some workable and effective legislation.

If a ban on traditional forms of hunting leads to overpopulation and starvation, or to the use of other methods of control which cause more suffering, then the law will have done more harm than good. Although the Hunting Act is just one year old (at the time of writing), there is already enough evidence to suggest that this is precisely what is happening. The most obvious manifestation of this, as far as foxes are concerned, is the increase in shooting and snaring in areas where fox-hunting is no longer practised, or now deemed ineffective as a form of control. Shooting undoubtedly leads to wounding; and snaring, which remains legal, can cause great suffering.

As a result of the Hunting Act, organised fox hunts are now wary of pursuing and killing animals which are suffering from diseases such as mange when they are following an artificial trail with a full pack of hounds. And in the West Country, deer hunts are finding it far more difficult to track down 'casualty deer' hit by vehicles when using two hounds, as the law now insists, rather than a dozen or more, as they did in the past. This means that deer which would formerly have been put out of their misery now linger longer. This, too, means that the Hunting Act is making matters worse, not better, from the point of view of animal welfare.

The Hunting Act is primarily concerned with just four species – fox, red deer, hare and mink – and it ignores the welfare of all other animals, both domestic and wild.[2] If the ban on hunting leads to greater predation of lambs, or more attacks on poultry, or increases the losses of ground-nesting birds, then again – as Webster puts it

– we shall have done more harm than good. The Hunting Act also fails to recognise that human beings are every bit as much part of the lived-in landscape as foxes and rabbits, sparrows and snipe. Legislation which fails to take into account the way in which farmers and others perceive the world around them is unlikely to achieve its goals. We need to recognise people's weaknesses as well as their strengths, and their motives for doing things, whether hunting foxes for pleasure, or conserving woodland to provide cover for wild mammals and birds.

It is all very well Professor Stephen Harris and his allies claiming that there is no need to control foxes. The reality is that a great many farmers believe, rightly or wrongly, that foxes do need to be controlled, and if they cannot be controlled one way, they will control them another.[3] Lord Burns suggested that in most areas the most humane way of killing foxes is lamping, which involves a marksman dazzling a fox with a bright light and killing it with a high-powered rifle. However, other methods are available to farmers too, and these, whether legal or illegal, will often be used. A sheep farmer in the Welsh hills, or high up in the Yorkshire Dales, is unlikely to worry too much about the niceties of the law when it comes to killing animals which he considers a threat to his liveli-hood. If the hunt is not allowed to kill his foxes and there are no lampers available, he will either take up his shotgun, or resort to the use of snares and possibly poison. And it will not only be the foxes that suffer, but all the other animals that are caught in snares or inadvertently poisoned.

By concentrating solely on the way in which individual animals die, and the manner of their death, the Hunting Act failed to recognise the complex relationship which exists between hunter and hunted, and the way in which this differs from the relationship between humans and animals when animals are seen simply in terms of the damage they do to livestock or crops. When animals are treated as pests, the aim is to kill as many as possible, and to expend the least effort doing so. A gun pack which is trying to rid a forestry plantation of foxes is not interested in selecting a few foxes, and leaving others so they can be pursued later; it will kill as many as possible. Likewise, a farmer who wishes to clear his barns of rats, whether with poison or dogs, hopes to transform his barns into a rat-free zone. With pest control, killing effectively, rather than humanely, tends to be the guiding principle, and a degree of suffering – often considerable suffering – is sanctioned by the law.[4]

The motives of those who hunt fox, deer, hare and mink are markedly different from those of the pest-controller. Everyone who follows hounds derives pleasure from the sport, even where there is a strong element of pest control, as there tends to be in upland areas with large populations of sheep. Many of those who follow these upland packs are farmers themselves. They want the hunts to kill foxes and keep the population down to an acceptable level, and many will call out the huntsman on 'lambing calls' to deal with rogue foxes, but few want to exterminate them completely, not least because they enjoy the camaraderie of the hunt and the relaxation it affords during the winter months.

Hunting is a form of wildlife management. It aims to keep populations of wild mammals below the level where they would be regarded as pests, and possibly subject to more brutal methods of control. Hunting depends on the goodwill of landowners. Landowners are prepared to tolerate some foxes and deer on their land, but not so many that they do significant damage. If the hunts fail to keep numbers down to a reasonable level, the landowners will either kill the animals themselves, or allow others to do it for them. It is in the interests of the hunt to manage fox and deer populations in a manner which satisfies landowners. It is also in the interests of the animals themselves. Ban hunting, and you deprive the fox and the deer, paradoxically, of one of their most powerful allies: the local hunt.

Once the hunt goes, the status of the fox, the deer and the hare immediately changes. The result will almost always be the same: foxes and other quarry will be killed in other ways, often causing more suffering, frequently by people who have little interest in maintaining a healthy population. Just look at what happened to the hare. After the Hunting Act came into force, and hare-coursing became illegal, over 8,000 hares were shot on a mere 10 coursing estates. Sports-minded estate owners no longer felt compelled to conserve hares now that coursing was banned. None of this should come as a surprise. The symbiotic relationship between hunter and hunted can be seen in many other places around the world. From my own experience, I think in particular of the elephant populations of Zimbabwe. From the point of view of peasant farmers, elephants are often a menace: they frequently trample their crops, knock over their flimsy homes, and occasionally kill those who get in their way. This has led to a continuous war between peasants and elephants – except in those areas where the elephants have a tangible value to hunters, and where the profits from safari hunting are shared with the villagers. In areas such as these, and I visited many during the 1990s, the villagers no longer look upon elephants as dangerous pests, to be killed by snares and poison, but as a source of income. They protect elephants from poachers and they even dig water holes for elephants, and for other species that have a value to hunters, and therefore to themselves, during times of drought. It was no coincidence that before President Mugabe plunged his country, and the countryside, into its current horrors, rural Zimbabwe had one of the healthiest populations of wildlife in Africa. This is not because the villagers recognised the animals' 'rights'. It reflected, rather, a relationship between man and nature which involved a system of careful exploitation and management mutually beneficial to both.[5] Precisely such a relationship exists here – or existed – between most organised hunts and their quarry.

The Middle Way Group has proposed a two-pronged approach to improve the welfare of all wild mammals in the countryside. This involves amending the Hunting Act to allow licensed hunting; and introducing new legislation which will make it an offence intentionally to cause undue suffering to any wild mammal under *any* circumstance.[6] This was the intention of the Wild Mammals (Protection) (Amendment) Bill, which was introduced in the House of Lords by Lord Donoughue in 2003 and in the House of Commons by Lembit Öpik in 2004. The Lords voted in favour of the new legislation. Anti-hunting MPs, however, blocked the Bill in the House of Commons. Although the Bill failed to become law, it provides a template for future legislation, and it has already received the backing of the majority of organisations which get their hands dirty in the practical management of the countryside, including the Countryside Alliance, the CLA and the National Farmers' Union (NFU).

The Bill seeks to amend the Wild Mammals (Protection) Act 1996. It will establish a new Authority, appointed by the secretary of state, and comprising members of organisations with proven expertise in the fields of countryside management, animal welfare and field sports, such as the Joint Nature Conservation Committee, the Universities Federation for Animal Welfare and the Council for Hunting Associations. The Authority will have the power to review existing codes of practice, or establish new codes of practice, for all activities which involve the control and management of wild mammals, from fox-hunting to shooting, coursing to snaring. By calling on expert opinion and relying on science-based evidence, the Authority will ensure that the codes of practice proscribe activities which cause undue suffering. For example, if the Authority receives definitive scientific proof that the final stages of a stag hunt cause undue suffering, it will be able to insist that the codes of practice be revised to reduce the length of the chase. If the Authority receives credible evidence that, say, certain shooting regimes cause high levels of wounding in foxes or other mammals, then it will recommend that these be proscribed by the relevant codes of practice.

Existing legislation which deals with the welfare of wild animals uses the term 'unnecessary cruelty'. This term is in many ways unsatisfactory. The word 'unnecessary' gives no indication of the degree of suffering; it could be trivial, or immense. Furthermore, whether something is necessary or not is open to debate. It could be argued that hunting, shooting and fishing are unnecessary; and the same could be said for rearing livestock and keeping pets. The word 'cruelty' is also unsatisfactory in this context, as it relates not so much to the animal which suffers, as the person who causes the suffering. It was for these reasons that Lord Donoughue and Lembit Öpik, in formulating their Bill, used the term 'undue suffering' rather than 'unnecessary cruelty'. The word 'undue' implies that activities can be measured against benchmarks or standards of animal welfare, some of which already exist and are currently in use for such things as licensing methods of trapping. Activities which fail to meet agreed benchmarks would not be licensed for use. By establishing an Authority which can take into account recent scientific developments, and improvements in our knowledge about animal welfare, this legislation will be much more fluid and flexible than its predecessors.

The new legislation will provide guidance about what hunting activities are acceptable, and which are not, and it will make recommendations about the codes of practice. However, hunting itself will be governed by separate legislation, which will involve either the repeal of the Hunting Act 2004 or its amendment. The new Act will also establish an independent Authority, similar in constitution to the Authority which will oversee the Wild Mammals (Protection) (Amendment) Act, and this Authority will be responsible for licensing hunting activities. The Middle Way Group suggests that all hunting activities would require a licence. In their applications, the hunters – they will range from large mounted packs of fox-hunters to individuals who wish to hunt rabbits with lurchers – would have to specify where they intended to hunt and how. The Authority would have the power to refuse licences, and revoke or suspend the licences of those who broke the relevant codes of conduct, or the specific conditions under which their licence had been granted. The Authority could draw on expert opinion, and its activities would be funded not by the taxpayer, but by licensees.

If the Wild Mammals (Protection) (Amendment) Bill, or similar legislation, becomes law, then anybody who witnesses an activity which they believe causes undue suffering will be able to take their case to the police, who can mount a prosecution if there is sufficient evidence. It will then be left up to the courts (rather than Parliament) to decide whether or not an act, or activity, has caused undue suffering.

The Wild Mammals (Protection) (Amendment) Bill was vigorously opposed by the RSPCA, IFAW, the League Against Cruel Sports and their friends in the animal rights movement. Their obsession with a hunting ban blinded them to the benefits this Bill could have brought to all wild mammals in the countryside. No doubt they will continue to oppose any efforts to reintroduce this or similar legislation, and so will the committed phalanx of pro-ban politicians, most of whom, incidentally, represent urban constituencies and know little or nothing about rural affairs. The likes of Dennis Skinner, Sir Gerald Kaufman, Peter Hain and Ann Widdecombe are not going to swallow their pride and admit they were wrong; that they were motivated, in part at least, by a contempt for those who enjoy an arcane rural pastime; that they failed to examine the evidence objectively.

I am not suggesting that the anti-hunting lobby has a monopoly on bigotry and prejudice. I can remember the time, not much more than a decade ago, when the individuals who spoke publicly for the hunting world were convinced of the rightness of their own cause, and contemptuously dismissive of those who opposed them. They gave the impression that they had a God-given right to do as they pleased, and they ignored legitimate concerns about certain hunting practices. However, unlike the anti-hunting lobby, the hunting world has begun to listen to its critics: many hunting people now accept that they should not be above the law, or their activities beyond public scrutiny. The most obvious outward manifestation of this changing attitude has been the recent appointment of Kate Hoey, the Labour MP for Vauxhall, as the chair of the Countryside Alliance.

Hoey understands that hunting is about much more than the pursuit and killing of wild animals. She realises that it is not so much a system of pest control – although there are elements of that – as a way of managing wildlife. It brings pleasure to those who hunt, but it also benefits the hunted species and the natural world in which they live. Hoey also recognises that animal welfare is important. Indeed, that is why she was one of the founder members of the Middle Way Group: she rejected the idea of a hunting ban, but she believed that hunting should be conducted under licence and overseen by an independent authority that can outlaw practices that cause undue suffering.

'If the Bill succeeds,' she told the House of Commons during the Second Reading of Michael Foster's Private Member's Bill to ban hunting, 'we shall make criminals of many law-abiding, decent citizens. That is bad legislation. It is intolerable and intolerant. It will do nothing to stop real cruelty and it will ruin the countryside.' The Foster Bill never reached the statute books, but the legislation which did is almost as bad. The sooner it is amended or repealed the better. In its place we need legislation which recognises that the welfare of animals, the well-being of people, and the richness and integrity of the natural world are inextricably linked.

NOTES

INTRODUCTION

1. Charles Clover, *Daily Telegraph*, 6 January 1996.

2. The All Party Parliamentary Middle Way Group estimated that the League Against Cruel Sports, IFAW and the RSPCA spent £30 million on anti-hunting campaigns in the UK between 1997 and 2002. This figure was never refuted.

3. Letter from Jackie Ballard, director-general of the RSPCA, to Lembit Öpik MP, 9 May 2005.

4. *Daily Telegraph*, 8 February 1997

5. *Fox-Hunting: Beyond the Propaganda*, by Charlie Pye-Smith, Wildlife Network, 1997

CHAPTER 1

1. The Political Animal Lobby, which has close ties with the International Fund for Animal Welfare (IFAW), had previously given donations to the three main parties, but on a much smaller scale, with the Labour Party receiving £50,000, the Conservatives £33,000 and the Liberal Democrats £20,000.

2. *The Times*, 1 March 2003

3. Letter to Lembit Öpik MP, 10 April 2002.

4. The Campaign for the Protection of Hunted Animals was formed in 1996 by the League Against Cruel Sports, the RSPCA and IFAW. In November 1998, it launched 'Deadline 2000,' a campaign to get the Government to deliver a ban by the end of the century. In January 2002, this was re-launched as 'Countdown to the Ban.'

5. This email was quoted by James Gray MP, Hunting Bill Select Committee, 13 February 2003.

6. DEFRA news release, 27 February 2003.

7. *Cruelty and utility: comments on principles and acceptability*, Game Conservancy Trust, 2002.

8. As above.

9. *Western Morning News*, 24 February 2004

10. BBC *Any Questions*, 23 October 2004

11. *Fox Control in the Countryside* by Jonathan Reynolds, Game Conservancy Trust, 2000.

CHAPTER 2

1. High Court of Justice Divisional Court, Case No: CO/835/2005; CO/2446/2005; CO/967/2005, 29 July 2005

2. *Welfare implications of culling red deer (Cervus elaphus)* by EL Bradshaw and P Bateson, 2000, *AnimalWelfare*, 9: 3-24.

3. As this chapter involves two professors called Harris, I have used their Christian names throughout to avoid confusion.

4. P Bateson and RC Harris, 2000, Contract 7 to the Burns Inquiry.

5. See www.vet-wildlifemanagement.org.uk *Bateson Then and Now*, compiled by Ian Addison

6. Letter to Charles Nunneley from Prof. Roger Harris, 2 November 2000.

7. Expert report by L.H.Thomas and W.R.Allen, High Court of Justice, Claim co/835/2005

8. *A Veterinary Opinion on Hunting with Hounds*, L.H.Thomas and W.R.Allen.

9. Letter from Charles Harding to J.Studholme, 5 May 2001.

10. *Is the fox a pest?* Robbie McDonald, Phil Baker and Stephen Harris, 1997. *How will a ban on hunting affect the British fox population?* Stephen Harris and Phil Baker, Campaign for the Protection of Hunted Animals, 1997.

11. *Shooting Times and Country Magazine*, 2 April 1998.

12. Game Conservancy Trust, Position Statement on the above, January 1998.

13. Letter from Terry Kreeger to the *Sunday Times*, unpublished.

14. Kreeger, T.J., Monson, D., Kuechle, V.B., Seal, U.S. and Tester, J.R. (1989) Monitoring heart rate and body temperature in red foxes (Vulpes vulpes). *Canadian Journal of Zoology*, 67, 2455-2458.

15. Kreeger, T.J., White, P.J., Seal, U.S. and Tester, J.R. (1990) Pathological responses of red foxes to foothold traps. *Journal of Wildlife Management*, 54, 147–160.

16. Harris and Baker provided a web reference: www.envirolink.org/arrs/essays/foxstdies.html. This is now redirected to www.animalconcerns.org.

17. Letter from Dr Terry Kreeger to the *Sunday Times*, unpublished.

18. Email from Dr Terry Kreeger, 6 December 2005.

19. www.huntinginquiry.gov.uk/evidence/kreeger.htm

20. In response to a letter from Lembit Öpik MP, representatives of IFAW, the League Against Cruel Sports and the RSPCA wrote, on 22 December 2003, 'the IFAW-funded study on wounding rates is currently undergoing peer review and awaiting publication.' Two years later, in another letter to Öpik, dated July 4th 2005, Professor Stephen Harris explained that he was addressing some minor points in his paper, and implied that it would soon be published.

21. Wounding rates in shooting foxes (*Vulpes vulpes*), by N.C.Fox, N.Blay, A.G.Greenwood, D.Wise and E.Potapov, *Animal Welfare*, 2005, Vol 14, No 2.

22. I say 'above ground,' because we do not know what levels of wounding occur when terriers are used to dig out foxes. Whether or not terrierwork causes suffering when conducted well – it certainly does when conducted badly – is open to debate. However, the very nature of the practice, which can be time-consuming and may involve the harrying of the fox underground, suggests that it will cause greater trauma than the killing of foxes by hounds above ground. Prior to the Hunting Act, around half the kills of organised hunts involve digging out. Many thousands more foxes are killed by terriermen and gamekeepers.

23. 'For the record I do not view Nick Fox as being a suitably qualified scientist. As far as I understand, his expertise is breeding hybrid designer falcons for rich Arabs, and I can find very little about his scientific achievements on any scientific abstracting service.' Letter from Stephen Harris to Lembit Öpik MP, 29 October 2003.

24. Letter from Stephen Harris to Peter Luff MP, 1 July 2003.

25. For the exchange of letters, see *Animal Welfare*, 2005, Vol 14, No 3, and 2006, Vol 15, No 1.

26. Baker and Stephen Harris ignored the fact that most rifle shooting takes place at night, when follow-up shots are less likely.

27. *Shooting of game/crippling/wounding*, J.Bertsden (ed) Ministry of Environment and Energy, Denmark, 1999.

28. Nick Fox et al, *Welfare Aspects of Shooting Foxes*, All Party Parliamentary Middle Way Group, 2003.

29. Letter from Stephen Harris to Peter Luff MP, 1 July 2003.

30. Here is one minor example of personal interest to me. Evidence was presented to both the Burns Inquiry and the Portcullis House hearings that 50,000 foxes were dug out using terriers and 10,000 killed by lurchers each

year. If you trace these figures back to their original home, you end up with a modest booklet called *Fox-hunting: Beyond the Propaganda*. I suppose I should be flattered to be quoted so widely in such august proceedings, but I pointed out in the booklet – as those who later quoted me failed to do in explicit terms – that these figures were speculative and 'as hard to refute as they are to support'. So a back-of-an-envelope calculation made one evening in the pub was subsequently translated, over a short period of time, into what amounted to established fact, to be cited by a Government ministry at one hearing, and by scientists (including Stephen Harris) at another.

31. Referee's Report by Stephen Harris for *Animal Welfare*, 19 August 2004.

CHAPTER 3

1. *Utility and cruelty – reasons to ban hunting with dogs*, Campaign for the Protection of Hunted Animals

2. 12 March 2001.

3. Letter from Douglas Batchelor to the *Daily Telegraph*, 28 January 2003.

4. Letter from Jim Barrington to the *Daily Telegraph*, 29 January 2003

5. Letter from Douglas Batchelor to Edward Marriage, 5 January 2000.

6. Letter from John Cooper, chairman of the League Against Cruel Sports, to Alun Michael MP, 18 June 2002.

7. Letter to *The Times*, 17 July 1996.

8. Ref High Court of Justice

9. *Fox Control in the Countryside*, by Jonathon Reynolds, Game Conservancy Trust, 2000.

10. *Managing British Mammals*, by David Macdonald et al, 2000, Wildlife Conservation Research Unit, Oxford University.

11. Letter from Jackie Ballard to Lord Donoughue, 8 April 2004.

12. Letter from Middle Way Group to RSPCA, IFAW and the League, 3 December 2003.

13. Response from RSPCA, IFAW and the League, 20 December 2003.

14. The League Against Cruel Sports were initially impressed by the Middle Way Group research. Douglas Batchelor, the chief executive began a letter to the *Daily Telegraph* thus on 7 June 2003: 'The important piece of new research that finds that shooting maims as many foxes as it kills…'

15. All Party Parliamentary Middle Way Group press release, 7 June 2005.

16. *Animal Welfare: Limping Towards Eden*, by John Webster, Blackwell, 2005

17. Letter from Peter Luff MP to Jackie Ballard, 17 August 2005.

18. *Welfare Aspects of Killing or Capturing Wild Vertibrates in Britain*, Nick Fox and Helen Macdonald, undated.

19. *Cruelty and Utility*, by Jonathan Reynolds, Game Conservancy Trust, 2002.

20. *Cruelty and Utility*, by Jonathan Reynolds, Game Conservancy Trust, 2002.

21. *Daily Telegraph*, 26 October 2002.

22. Farming Today, BBC Radio 4, 17 June 2003.

23. RSPCA's Declaration of Animal Rights was announced in 1979 in its *Policies on Animal Welfare*.

24. *Who Cares for Animals? 150 Years of the RSPCA*, A. Brown, Heinemann, 1974.

25. Letter to *The Times*, 12 September 2005.

26. Survey conducted by Brian Fanshawe of the Council of Hunting Associations on behalf of the Masters of Foxhounds Association, 1 December 2005.

27. 'Are Political Motives Concealing the Facts?' by Jeffrey Olstead, *Shooting Times*, 19 June 2003.

CHAPTER 4

1. Professor Webster believes that the killing of animals for sport is morally objectionable. However, he stresses that it is of no consequence whatsoever to the animal whether we derive pleasure from the act of killing, or experience disgust, or allocate the task of killing to someone else and try not to think about it.

2. However, the Hunting Act potentially affects every dog owner whose dog chases, say, a mouse, a squirrel or a hare.

3. Professor Stephen Harris and his colleagues conducted a questionnaire survey of farmers and land managers which found that approximately a third would increased their levels of shooting, and to a lesser extent snaring, if there was a ban on hunting with dogs. See: The current and future management of wild mammals hunted with dogs in England and Wales, PCL White et al, *Journal of Environmental Management*, 67, 2, February 2003.

4. For example, DEFRA noted in its 1997 *Assessment of Fully Approved Vertebrate Control Agents*: 'As severe discomfort, which can last for several days, occurs in a large proportion of all the reported studies, anti-coagulant rodenticides must be regarded as being markedly inhumane.'

5. This system of wildlife management, known by the acronym CAMPFIRE, has been widely written about. See, for example, *The Wealth of Communities*, by Charlie Pye-Smith, Grazia Borrini-Feyerabend and Richard Sandbrook, Earthscan, 1994.

6. Lord Burns, whom the anti-hunting organisations have been so fond of quoting in their favour, came to much the same conclusions as the Middle Way Group. During a debate in the House of Lords, he suggested that there was a way forward 'through a combination of licensed hunting and further reform of animal welfare legislation'.